Love! Love. Love?

VOLUME 1

Dedications

I would like to dedicate this book to God first and foremost the author and the finisher of my life's story, but also to Keshon Nowlin. May his soul rest in peace; my handsome little cousin who has gone to be with the lord. Far too soon, he had such a bright future ahead with a pure heart and good intentions. He was loved by all; Taken away before he was able to give Love his all. However, he wasn't short of receiving all that love had to offer from his mom, younger siblings, grandparents and many more. I dedicate this Book to you my "Little Big Cousin" whom I love whole heartedly and miss very much, I hope I can make you proud. We are all down here shouting "LONG LIVE KESHON!" I am so grateful to have known you and shared in your moments and got the chance to see a glimpse of the man your mom raised and that we knew you would be. Your legacy speaks for your character and we will make sure everyone knows how great you are. And finally, to each struggle, set back, and downfall I ever faced, I thank you because in the end, I became a stronger me a wiser me. With each story that you read, you won't just read it, you will feel it. Don't just feel but know that you can overcome it. So, I dedicate this book to all of my Ups and Downs. You did not and were not able to keep me down!

Contents

Introduction

This book has been long overdue. Ironically, it is something I have been working on for over half my life, and yet a piece of me knows that it will never be finished. I used to write just as a pass time to express myself because it was easier to speak to a blank page versus someone who can run their mouth passing judgment or sharing their opinion when I never asked. In any case, you will see my mistakes, growth, hurt, and pain. That is when I'm most creative however, don't think you know me because the hurt and pain did help mold me. It turned me into a new me. As you read, I was sure to add in some hyperboles, similes, and a haiku or 15 if you know what I mean. You will witness the raw untouched thoughts from my adolescent mind through the stages of me learning myself, along with overcoming fears and conquering mountains that appeared to me as giants at the time. As you read, I hope you will come to appreciate the new Butterfly that is me, opposed to the tortured caterpillar that I thought no one cared for or could see. I am currently working from my iPhone as my one-year old baby girl lies here asleep on me; a whole different type of love entirely. Some old and some new, some healed, but most cut deep. I will always rise to the occasion and you will see. Enjoy this piece of me, and if no one has told you lately, just know I love you, I care for you, I pray for you more than I pray for myself, you are Special, and you do matter!

(Don't categorize me and put me in a box. They try and call me urban, fiction, religious
..... add scripture to match times?)

You'll realize a pattern to my writing. Often times, my mind wouldn't rest. Heartbreak and mind crazed days fueled my creative pain. My muse was life's tight reign and rings that sometimes held me till the feeling of almost all ending breath. But from that pain grew onto the most beautiful Butterfly that landed on an even more beautiful rose.
There are many different types of love. Whether it be real love or not, easy or hard, infinite or inevitable, Agape or Eros. As a human race, we often love blindly and recklessly, even if it consumes us. Everyone feels love on

5

some level, healthy or unhealthy, in any manor or form. This love can develop on a business, platonic, or more intimate level. I have felt "Lust" and have confused it for love. I have loved, lost, and finally understand the saying "better to have loved and lost, then to never have loved at all." Once you become a parent, you will understand that saying as well or just in due time as you mature, experience life, and grow. I have learned that my greatest accomplishments come from my failures. And it is in those moments or seasons when I learned and gained wisdom, knowledge, and truth. As a creative, I personally get my inspiration from hurt and pain. My best work is revealed when I am under pressure, mad, hurt, or angry. I know that isn't a good thing, and I clearly have some soul-searching to do and therapy sessions that I might need to attend, but as for now or then, it was and has been the only time I was able to produce my most meaningful works with the most substance. A lot of times, we as people, male and female alike, hide our true selves in fear of rejection, abandonment, or even to benefit our own selfish needs and personal agendas amongst other reasons. It is not always about "speaking up" or "not taking crap" from someone or dealing with a certain situation. It is also about being an empath and logically thinking as a better you and a whole. For instance, I may think about saying something, but thinking before I speak allowed me to take into consideration the effect that my words may have after they have been spoken. I ask myself, "Would the outcome be good or bad? Would my comment, statement, words benefit me or that person or situation in a positive way afterwards? Is my only reason to say or not to say something out of fear?"

Those are the questions and conversations we often have with ourselves; I know I have. What you will read is what I Wish I would have said in some past moments. Sometimes I, did sometimes I didn't; maybe it was fear, maybe it wasn't. Above all, that version of me was trying to move on and rise above the situation trying to rise above all of hurt and pain without holding onto negative energy.

There is no process for me or a specific muse unless you look at pain as my muse; the very thing that motivates me and gives birth to my writings. Very rarely will you see writing about just "being" solely and "intentionally," but hey, that is just me. A broken heart lost love or lies followed by tears. When a traumatic situation happens, it leaves me in a stage or phase that doesn't last always, but when it comes, it hits hard and unable to express myself directly to the person, I communicate best with my pen. What you will see, read, and experience the way I love. The way I was loved. The way love hurt me. The way I questioned love. The way I craved love. The way I turned lust into love. The way I yearned for love.

My most inner thoughts in a few lines that are right-to-the-point, quick, raw and razor sharp.

Ways to Love and there Meanings:
Type of Love

Ask yourself these questions as you read or when you place yourself in the story and get wrapped up in these moments. And know that it is ok to allow yourself to love and be loved again. Do you know how to love properly? Have you been Loved properly? What type of love do you often find yourself in? Are you afraid to love? What love do you want for your future self, what is your Love language, now that you know the different types of love that you can receive?

1. Eros

Eros is sexual or passionate love and is the type most akin to our modern construct of romantic love. In Greek myth, it is a form of madness brought about by one of Cupid's arrows. The arrow breaches us and we 'fall' in love, as did Paris with Helen, leading to the Trojan War and the downfall of Troy and much of the assembled Greek army. In modern times, Eros has been amalgamated with the broader life force, something akin to Schopenhauer's will, a fundamentally blind process of striving for survival and reproduction. Eros has also been contrasted with Logos, or Reason, and Cupid painted as a blindfolded child.

2. Philia

The hallmark of philia, or friendship, is shared goodwill. Aristotle believed that a person can bear goodwill to another for one of three reasons: that he is useful; that he is pleasant; and, above all, that he is good, that is, rational and virtuous. Friendships founded on goodness are associated not only with mutual benefit but also with companionship, dependability, and trust.

For Plato, the best kind of friendship is that which lovers have for each other. It is a philia born out of Eros, and that in turn feeds back into Eros to strengthen and develop it, transforming it from a lust for possession into a shared desire for a higher level of understanding of the self, the other, and the world. In short, philia transforms Eros from a lust for possession into an impulse for philosophy.

Real friends seek together to live truer, fuller lives by relating to each other authentically and teaching each other about the limitations of their beliefs and the defects in their character, which are a far greater source of error than mere rational confusion: they are, in effect, each other's therapist—and in that much it helps to find a friend with some degree of openness, articulacy, and insight, both to change and to be changed.

3. Storge

Storge ('store-gae'), or familial love, is a kind of philia pertaining to the love between parents and their children. It differs from most philia in that it tends, especially with younger children, to be unilateral or asymmetrical. More broadly, storge is the fondness born out of familiarity or dependency and, unlike Eros or philia, does not hang on our personal qualities. People in the early stages of a romantic relationship often expect unconditional storge, but find only the need and dependency of Eros, and, if they are lucky, the maturity and fertility of philia. Given enough time, Eros tends to mutate into storge.

4. Agape

Agape is universal love, such as the love for strangers, nature, or God. Unlike storge, it does not depend on filiation or familiarity. Also called charity by Christian thinkers, agape can be said to encompass the modern concept of altruism, defined as unselfish concern for the welfare of others. Recent studies link altruism with a number of benefits. In the short term, altruism leaves us with a euphoric feeling—the so-called 'helper's high'. In the longer term, it is associated with better mental and physical health, as well as longevity. At a social level, altruism serves as a signal of cooperative intentions, and also of resource availability and so of mating or partnering potential.

9

It also opens up a debt account, encouraging beneficiaries to reciprocate with gifts and favors that may be of much greater value to us than those with which we feel able to part. More generally, altruism, or agape, helps to build and maintain the psychological, social, and, indeed, environmental fabric that shields, sustains, and enriches us. Given the increasing anger and division in our society, and the state of our planet, we could all do with quite a bit more agape.

5. Ludus

Ludus is playful or uncommitted love. It can involve activities such as teasing and dancing, or more overt flirting, seducing, and conjugating. The focus is on fun, and sometimes also on conquest, with no strings attached. Ludus relationships are casual, undemanding, and uncomplicated but, for all that, can be very long-lasting. Ludus works best when both parties are mature and self-sufficient. Problems arise when one party mistakes ludus for Eros, whereas ludus is in fact much more compatible with philia.

6. Pragma

Pragma is a kind of practical love founded on reason or duty and one's longer-term interests. Sexual attraction takes a back seat in favor of personal qualities and compatibilities, shared goals, and making it work. In the days of arranged marriages, pragma must have been very common. Although unfashionable, it remains widespread, most visibly in certain high-profile celebrity and political pairings. Many relationships that start off as Eros or ludus end up as various combinations of storge and pragma. Pragma may seem opposed to ludus, but the two can co-exist, with the one providing a counterpoint to the other. In the best of cases, the partners in the pragma relationship agree to turn a blind eye—or even a sympathetic eye, as in the case of Simone de Beauvoir and Jean-Paul Sartre, or Vita Sackville-West and Harold Nicholson.

7. Philautia

Philautia is self-love, which can be healthy or unhealthy. Unhealthy self-love is akin to hubris. In Ancient Greece, a person could be accused of hubris if he placed himself above the gods, or, like certain modern politicians, above the greater good. Many believed that hubris led to destruction, or nemesis. Today, hubris has come to mean an inflated sense of one's status, abilities, or accomplishments, especially when accompanied by haughtiness or arrogance. As it disregards truth, hubris promotes injustice, conflict, and enmity.

Healthy self-love is akin to self-esteem, which is our cognitive and, above all, emotional appraisal of our own worth relative to that of others. More than that, it is the matrix through which we think, feel, and act, and reflects and determines our relation to ourselves, to others, and to the world.
Self-esteem and self-confidence do not always go hand in hand. In particular, it is possible to be highly self-confident and yet to have profoundly low self-esteem, as is the case with many performers and celebrities.

People with high self-esteem do not need to prop themselves up with externals such as income, status, or notoriety, or lean on crutches such as alcohol, drugs, or sex. They are able to invest themselves completely in projects and people because they do not fear failure or rejection. Of course, they suffer hurt and disappointment, but their setbacks neither damage nor diminish them. Owing to their resilience, they are open to growth experiences and relationships, tolerant of risk, quick to joy and delight, and accepting and forgiving of themselves and others.

In closing, there is, of course, a kind of porosity between the seven types of love, which keep on seeping and passing into one another. For Plato, love aims at beautiful and good things, because the possession of beautiful and good things is called happiness, and happiness is an end-in-itself. Of all beautiful and good things, the best, most beautiful, and most dependable is truth or wisdom, which is why Plato called love not a god but a philosopher:
He whom love touches not walks in darkness.

Chapter 1

03/16/2014

I feel empty
Like there's a closed door
I'm trying to get through and a darkness
that's so filling

My mind wandering and heart racing,
bringing tears to my eyes
and I feel like I can't take it

Don't wanna be caged in, lord help me,
don't let the devil take me!
I have to fight, hold on,
and kick to make it

But honestly, I can say, I'm feeling caged in
Empty,Scared and alone
But with no one around to hold,

I drop to my knees. Fold my hands 'n begin to
pray a prayer 'n call out,
"Oh God, just Help me!"

I wonder if he hears my cries,
I believe he does because he saved me
from a fight 'n the battle of my life against cancer,
and I WON

Only GOD can do that
But now I feel as though I'm on the run

Trying to get away, run away from myself,
get away 'n be free, and just run to some help
Just away from the Empty. Cold. Sad.
Scared. Mess and Loneliness
So I call out unto God, and

I have FAITH that he will answer 'n
supply my every need
GOD, my lord, 'n Jesus Christ;
he is ALL I need!

9:30PM

03/09/2014

My Heart. My Love
I miss YOU, each day wondering
how life would be with YOU
My Heart. My Love. My Smile

I miss YOU, wish I could be with YOU.
Constantly on my mind and
it's You I think of

Just letting you know,
wherever you are in the world tonight,
My Love My Heart

You're missed and
I'm sending you a Secret Kiss

1:36AM

03/21/2014

I just want to keep you uplifted!

13

I believe in you and I Love you
Forever your Lady.....

Do like a mini per gaming event in the clubhouse.
Shots in the house 'n more after,
Or just call it the per game Peep Show 'n

keep music playing
Once we leave for a few minutes

12:49AM

04/13/2014

My thoughts are too loud
Intuition ignored 'n Buried
10 feet down!

Heartbreak 'n sorrow holds the crown
Sadness drowned out by the quiet
Eye lids heavy and tears start to flow

2:45AM

05/18/2014

I want to lay down with you every night,
Under the nights sky,

And be the one you want to wake up to,
morning rise
Jasmine

2:47AM

06/24/2014

I don't know when it was the last time I made love...
It probably was peaceful, sensual, enjoyable....
I remember what it was like, faintly,
but still reminiscent of all things, touch.....
Sound and sight.....
Whether it be day or night...
Never shed a tear, just smiled inside and out...

You touched my soul for that moment, and we both took Flight, Uplifting and intertwined between two lives....
I smile as I write....

This was a happy moment in my life, and I usually just write about how heavy my heart feels and how nothing is right. .....
But it was good to feel loved and wanted...
The last Day when we Made Love.

7:51PM

06/24/2014

I have words and they make thoughts!!
My thoughts are no better than yours,

But I hope my words will forever live
And make an everlasting noise!!!!

8:52PM

07/11/2014

I wonder...

15

Who is she, the girl you named her Z
or whoever she may be?
But then again, why should I care?

Maybe she gives you what you need,
loves you better than me
You stick around because you
love the inside of me,

But not knowing that internal scar still bleeds.
I wonder...Why do I care?

What makes it any better or so hard to leave?
Maybe it's the slight infatuation you had (have) over me.
I wonder why I care?

Why when I look 'n see your time occupied by someone new?
Does it hurt when there's already someone else calling me boo?

I wonder why it hurts, just the
thought of you with someone new
Even though I know, as of right now, you and
I are pretty much through

I wonder!! I wonder if you'll get it together
and treat her better
I wonder if my love wasn't enough,
if you hadn't of destroyed our trust.

I wonder why I care when I found someone new?
Things just aren't the same, but you and I both knew

2:59AM

07/12/2014

I'm faithful no matter the distance

16

But it seems you weren't compliant or Consistent....

10:33PM

07/15/2014

My first love became my first heartbreak
We met a few years ago,
but that part of us ended today
My first love became my first heartbreak
When it happened, the pain was so
sharp like a wooden stake

Tears began to run down my face
I wasn't certain of what words I would say...

11:05PM

07/16/2014

The silence is the worst
A car ride
A crowded room

A single line out of a verse
No matter the place, my mind and heart
Currently don't speak.

I just want to be at peace
Feel my heart's release
At ease with no stress. Beating freely

1:31AM

07/21/2014

I'm left standing here with a blank face 'n black tears
I can't help but to compare everybody to you
For so long, you were all that I knew

The best parts of you are what stole
my heart and kept me too
I remember staring in ya dark brown eyes thinking,
"Damn he's so fine."

I loved the feeling of knowing you were all mine
Until that day, my heart started to cry...
Black tears

You were no longer mine.
But still somehow,
I managed to hold on and put up a fight

You were everything I wanted,
you taught me about myself 'n I loved it
Now I can't wait to erase what almost feels like hate

Misty eyes, cloudy thoughts,
jumbled words and a broken...
That cries Black tears
Black tears, black tears

11:31AM

07/22/2014

I'm just so sick of people dying
Why can't you come back to me!?

We can live in this hateful world together, happily
As long as you're by my side

4:05PM

18

I went back to that place for the first time the other day
It stung really bad, like shattered glass in my face

I couldn't bring myself to walk through those sliding doors
Because I knew I still wouldn't see you anymore

My eyes tear up at the thought of your absence
But I still smile just thinking of your laughter

Your warm hugs and assertive embrace
You were such a woman filled with style and grace

Kind hearted and always knew what to say
A tear fell down, but you're no longer here to wipe it away!

We really miss you Aunt, I guess that's all I have to say.
Our Angel in the sky now. Rest. In. Peace.
While we pray!

8:57PM

Chapter 2

07/23/2014

I sat there thinking of words to say...
But then I realized my actions aren't the same

Unsure of what to say,
But I know that my words,

Or your words, can come out just the same
Don't feel inferior, jump out there

9:10PM

07/25/2014

At a time when I was down almost at my lowest
I just stopped 'n looked around
I knew the only sane thing to do was to fall to my knees and cry unto
you!

Father God, I thank you, for you are my strength and this I knew
I wasn't always sure of what to do, but in my time of need I knew it was
best to call you

2:23AM

07/27/2014

I met a girl...
Not the twirly girly girl type, but I met a girl
She had the cutest Swag along with nice hair
I never spoke

Just patiently waiting 'n looking from a distance
It was something different brand-new, she just caught my eye...
Had me thinking a thing or two!

But I met a girl and when we finally spoke,
I didn't blush, but I could almost feel my nerves choke
Smiling with the loudest grin

I couldn't help it, even when I tried to hold it in
I met a girl and I love her name
I'm just here existing not really expecting anything
But I met a girl, 'n for the first time I called her Bae

I met this girl 'n I wonder if, when, or how things will change
I met a girl 'n she makes me feel some type of way.
Anyway, that's all I wanted to say,
gotta get back to texting Bae

11:21PM

07/31/2014

Heard our song, ya old ringtone
That night I think I cried myself to sleep
I used to love you, believing you'd set me free

'Cause I couldn't do this thing called without you loving me
"Dangerously in Love" used to be my mindset.

1:39AM

08/04/2014

Second date
It went down like a delicious piece of cake
But she didn't bite the cake, no
we didn't hit (that) it right away...

Second date
"Got damn", is all I can say; eleven hours face to face
Time spent don't never seem like a waste
When she's gone, I miss her smile 'n her face...

Second date
I can't wait to get a better taste of her,
Eyes and into that mind.
How beautiful she looked

Made my heart beat flutter with just one look
I should've taken a picture,
to throw on the book (Facebook)

Second date
You might as well say she reached third base
A few more hours 'n she just might get a taste
Waiting and waiting impatiently for our next date

2:15PM

08/04/2014

So, you say you didn't want to get shot down...
What made you think I would shoot you down....?
You like talking to me all day? Cause if not I'll stop..?

So do you like girly girls or what....?
Sneakers or heels for your girl....?

Nike's or Jordan's....?
New Balance or Vans....?
Light skin or dark skin....?

Do you think I'm too assertive,
or do you like more assertiveness....?
Are you the aggressor or

22

aggressive type in your relationships....?

What turns you on....?
What is a turn off or pet peeve....?
Craziest thing you've done....?
What's something crazy you wanna do....?
(Was talkin' 'bout you) You got people jealous...
Check you out....

Would you say you love first or fall first..?
Fall in love or love....?
Do you cuddle after sex?

4:25PM

08/04/2014

This one right here
Makes my heart skip a beat, or race,
Not because of fear,

But the agonizing anticipation till
we reach our next destination

A trip we take just by riding each other
on an innate (natural) deeper rate
My infatuation is beyond

11:02PM

08/05/2014

I have thoughts of you and me
Like when we finally touch, it'll be explosive
Chest to chest, so soft 'n smooth as we lay 'n caress

I imagine your hands in mine and

23

you ever so lightly tempting me
Staring in each others eyes to intensify the ride

You would handle me oh so sweetly
while still giving me all of what I need?
The way you love is sensually;
as if I could feel your soul speak to me
I pictured you as the one inside and surrounding me
The one holding me so close 'n intimately

5:11AM

08/05/2014

I usually just write to myself
But I guess I'm like Drake,
I decide to share with someone else
Hope you like. This one is titled

"My New High"

It's something about chu
I don't wanna scare you away or frighten you,
But damn I really like you

It's something about chu
Maybe it's the way you walk, talk and smile
Maybe it's ya personality and laidback cool style
Or maybe it's when I look into your eyes and stare,
and you never blink,
you just stay right there

With your beautiful brown eyes and
soft skin that drives me wild
Or maybe the way I picture your
hands caressing my body
As if were intertwined or united

24

It's something about you
Like a first time high that
I can't get through
I'm infatuated with you and all you do

Addicted to this high, like the highest ride
I'm not obsessed 'n I'm not crazy,
I'm just riding this high cause it feels amazing
It's something about chu and
I don't even know what cha name is,
I guess it's time I start turning the pages.

3:31PM

08/10/2014

I just want you to fuck my mind,
ease my thoughts and do my body right!
Please me in every way,
excite me through touch sound and sight.

If anything, let ya body feel light while
I massage you with my mouth and
take you on flight

Erotically taming you while still
leaving parts of the beast out
I just wanna run away with you, baby

Can you follow me now unleveled,
compelling like a hellion?

1:21AM

Chapter 3

08/15/2014

Damn, shorty bad...
Not bad bad, but like 4th quarter standing a
t 1st down with no shoulder pads...

But wait, she plays ball, so maybe
I should rephrase that...
2nd half, 4th quarter, 15 second,
Kobe shook 'em, cumin up clutch, 'n then...

He took it! Swoosh, "he made it".
She made me think we were kinda dating...
But I ain't gonna say Sh**,
we just going keep flowin' 'n rockin'
like a hit playlist...

We like it and the way it is,
I just thought I should say this....
She got my attention kinda heavy, 'n all I can say is...
She like my lor Bae and I think I will stay with....
Hmm, maybe I should rethink this
through 'n then play it....

But either way, she got me
feeling faded high up in the clouds....
'n I can take it. First time feeling this way and...

Words usually come out tainted,
but with you, everything is changing....
I can't say I don't like to think

I'm going for the Goal like Michael Jordan that is....

Honestly idk what I'm doing,
I never before wrote like this or had these fears....
But this time around, I guess,
is the practice round......

Got me writing 'n rapping like
I'm some type of wonder kid....
I don't usually do this here.....

Be all happy writing shit down 'n
enjoying this shit or be good at it...
My most powerful words come
through when I'm hurt 'n broken down....

But I feel uplifted 'n on solid ground.....
Everything is new this time around....
Fresh air, new scene, we never predicted this here....

But all's well that ends well...
And if we keep it going like an engine belt
or the first kiss that made me melt...
Well, I think we'll be good.....

No titles, just enjoying one another, and it feels good....
Okay, enough, got me all mushy 'n shit! .....
Told you man, I don't usually do this....

Met her 'n she switched the game up,
gave my life a new twist.....
'N I can't say I'm not liking it.
When I'm older....

I'm sure she'll be a part of the Reminisce....
A thought or two filled with bliss 'n a few nudes...
But like 'shad said, "you knew....."

Okay, okay, I'm done.....

I'm through, but she still texting me, 'n
on my mind like a plate of good food....
Oh yeah, I like to eat too! Hopefully you didn't catch it.....
Wouldn't want you to feel not accepted...
Of me, but Truthfully I DON'T CARE....
Either way, I'ma keep doing me! .....

3:55AM

09/02/2014

Why mess up a good thing when
everything is so sweet?
Sad faces 'n feelings misplaced.
If you wanted more, then why not say?

I feel as though we had a good thing,
but you just walked away
So now I'm like what to say?

Where to go? Who to call Bae?
I feel as though you left me and
threw me away

2:05AM

09/06/2014

Damn, I miss you!!!
It's not a day I don't think
about you at least once!!!
I try stop but my mind n
heart both want parts!!!
It hurt me to my heart the
fact that you didn't say bye!!!

Thought we were better than that.
But any who!!!
I doubt if I send this to you,
just sitting here thinking like,
"fuck these niggas!!!
I'm on my shit now!!!"

Just wish I could lay in your arms
one last time or feel the realest love!!!
That we once had right before the fold!!!
We did good till the storm hit!!!

Anyway, this is just my way of
telling my mind you're really gone!!!
So just let go! But I guess I just have to
wait 'n let time tell or heal!!!
You know how the saying goes!!!
So, I wish you the Best! To a friend I used to know!!!

7:40PM

09/08/2014

In the part he came out the room while
I was on the other side,
looked, did a fake wave

I walked past, saw her laying there naked
He left the door open.
Then left for class.

I cried.
Then dragged her ass,
threw her out naked.

9:42AM

Why do I feel this way?
Why do you still have a hold on me?
Why can't my heart 'n mind be free?
I saw you tweet, but it wasn't about me

I'm really starting to hate you
Because I'm always feeling incomplete.
Like, you don't deserve anything
because I was the best,
But yet you keep looking for the rest

Bet she don't hold you down
Bet she can't put it down.
Bet your mom keep her around
Damn, I really hate you
Cause I bet you could care less about
who I date boo

'N yet, I still shed a tear over the
memories of me and you Fix it Jesus.
I want nothing more than to forget you

My past, my first, the love, the hurt,
I just wish I never knew you

Cause this hurt right here, is like agony and
it's constantly knocking at my door
So yeah, I guess it's true

I hate you, because I still love you.
Because I want you
Because I can't get you out of my head and
I need to Back to work I go

Growing on my own without you
I no longer wish you the best, just wish
I didn't know you.

09/08/2014

Why do I put myself through this?
The constant back 'n forth; like I'm stupid
He couldn't even say I miss you back or IMY,
Guess I'm the stupid in love one over you

Well guess what? After this boo,
fuck my feelings, and that includes you too!
I hate seeing your name pop up on the screen
I gotta get over you at all costs, no matter what I do.
'Cause you been stopped loving me,
so why should I love you?

Like a match to a fuse
Our flame went out like the candles you blew
Up in flames; red, yellow, 'n blue
Were the colors my heart bled for you?

But that's long gone now,
so what's left of it is out of use
I gotta get these thoughts out my head,
and feelings out my chest

I wish they could all be compressed
because I'm starting to feel depressed
I just want to be loved 'n rest.
But I'll fake 'n put up a fight since I can't rest

So, fuck love and you for making me feel like
I have nothing left

31

I curse you for constantly staying on my
mind like you want me

But believe me, love will trick you,
and it ain't funny
My first love my first heartbreak

09/15/2014

Do you remember my first time..?
It was with you
You were my first, but I wasn't yours
I remember every detail so vividly.

You and I, me and you
You inside of me, sliding through me
Oh Baby, do you feel me?

'Cause lately, I don't even know who you are,
Like you ain't really feeling me
We go back and forth

And when I'm speaking, it's
as if you still don't hear me
I wanna scream out, but it's not okay
You reached my soul, I reacted,

And you tossed my insides like a bad Salad
What did I ever do to deserve such bad treatment?
When all I ever did was love you?

My heart bleeds for you with permanent torture,
scars, 'n bruises that need
more than time to be fixed

2:11PM

32

09/19/2014

I still think of how you made my body feel
How our Souls connected,
and the screaming and scratches got hectic

I miss the shakes and water works we used to make
Pass the physical,
but spiritual and intellectual

You brought me closer to GOD and helped
ease my mind.3 months out, '
n my heart still ain't healed

You were my partner 'n lover—
my protector and cover
Good times 'n bad, we made
through like a breeze

I'd like to salute your patience;
you were man enough to wait,
But childish enough to take the bait

Yeah, you're a man, so I just still can't fade it
Let me go before my head starts to pound 'n
I can't take it

3:36PM

09/28/2014

She's in Love with my Mind;
We connected through time
He loves my insides

5:24AM

10/07/2014

He told me I was something that
he never knew he wanted,
But was exactly what he needed
But in the end, yeah...The end.

There's always an End
He ended up being nothing but a dreamer,
a big talker, small walker

Guess he didn't mean it
Made me laugh, made me smile;
I just enjoyed having him around

9:09AM

10/07/2014

So, my heart got screwed up
'N after that, every nigga's luck was up

You mess wit me, you bet not fuck up
Time is money 'n if you waste my time,
you gon owe me more than a few dimes

9:25AM

Chapter 4

(Soooo church was yesterday)

I know, understand,
Why I/we often times generate or produce work;
My thoughts in the earliest parts of the morning
Whether you're a believer or not, we as people,
"human beings",

Are made up of Body, Mind, Spirit/Intellect, Soul
As you sleep or rest, the part of you that's sleeping,
is your Body; that of flesh
While your spirit man, never sleeps
And if you pray before going to sleep,
as you get physical rest,

Your spirit and intellect are renewed and enlightened
Sometimes, so much that you are awakened,
If not fresh with insight and ideas upon your weakening.

10/21/2014

I'm on a path to happiness,
a path to inner peace

As I am in search of myself,
I realize how God is constantly moving me

In and out of the way of those which serve no purpose
Forever is not enough,

but I still long for your presence and
tender touch

35

Touch of the word and how brilliantly...

10/06/2014

Three nights;
Four days
The time quickly faded when you're falling
for or in like with the love or thought of...

Won't throw out titles, it makes things insane
Just know that I share your pain

When you're no longer there to fill in the silence,
and you start to feel pain

But hold onto that last kiss.
As if it was lingering

I like your eyes; you like my lips
I laid on your chest; you held my hips
It was undefined love,

so we just secretly call it bliss
Hidden in the shade until we're
able to block the Sun's rays

Yes, that was a metaphor for hiding our
secret looks, lip locks, long hugs, text messages,
and secret thoughts

But what's done in the dark must come to the light.
Until then,

We're fine with just existing in the Night
Until next time we meet, hold onto my lip

The one you like to bite!

11/10/2014

So, I met this guy...
And I just can't help but stare in his eyes
A beautiful smile and he hugs me so tight
I love the way he's into me...

It's like I'm his new high
I just hope we're both able to control the ride
The ride that's been undefined, no title, no tears, don't cry

I'm sitting here at this table and he's wondering why...
Honestly, I don't know, there's just this feeling inside...
But I can obviously see what he can't hide
A secret he found in me! My boo to be!

1:27AM

11/14/2014

White Roses

He gave me flowers
They were Roses
"Why aren't they RED?" I asked

He replied, "When you came into my life, I
began to see better

Red reminded me of being under the weather
no love just cloudy days with no cover
You came into my life and
made all the rain go away

37

" I replied, "How sweet of you

Do you know that everything happens for a reason?
And if this works, I'll be around longer than a season"

He smiled 'n grinned, with eyes so innocent,
I just had to let him in

He was a beautiful man and he called me his queen
My silence filled the air.
His Kiss was so debonair

Together, we worked, 'n so we stayed right there,
with the sun shinning on my white Roses

"PURE", is what he told me
I giggled, but he began to hold me
2 months, and this man already knows me
A white rose to represent our secret Love!

12:29PM

11/15/2014

I like you.
Shoot I may even love you, I keep saying how
I don't want to hurt you

But I just picture your heart being so fragile
But in the end, I have to protect myself
because my heart still has permanent wounds

I want to love you 'n give you my all
But to be honest, my ex keeps interfering with our calls
He's no good for me.

And you're the perfect man, I know you can be

38

I'm just being honest, so I hope you don't fault me!

To be honest, I think you're perfect and it amazes me
I can't explain the hold that my ex has over me
But I'm fighting to be with you,
the man that I know wants me
Our connection was Mental, Emotional

Beyond physical, but still Electrical
When we're together, everything is all good

So, I guess I have to make the decision
to disconnect from an unhealthy connect

I don't know if it's my heart or my brain,
but I can't deny still wanting him

Or, could it just be the thought of
my past knowing him
Either way, he could never be you,
make me smile, or feel how I do

When I stare into your eyes,
I feel beautiful; you chose me, which was a first
I can't lie, I used to try 'n hide
when standing next to her, but
it's like you saw me through the dark

Like a flower blooming in May
I think we can work because
we have this effortless urge, to see, hear,
Be near, and want one another

A love strong enough to bend as well as
Bloom in the cold months when I'm not home
Just hold on till I come home and make

wherever you are our own personal home
In spite of all other feelings,
roz here is where I wanna stay!

11/17/2014

Will you be my..?
I ask you this question to see if you say yes.
It's not a test, I just hope your answer is "yes!"
Will you be my...Date?

I'll pick you up around 8, open your door,
Even fix your plate
Make every second of every moment count
Will you be my..?

I just want you to feel special because you're my Date
Say yes, and I won't be late, we'll dance the night
away even if we have to fake

I promise you won't have to wait, another epic night
since we've only been on one date
Our time together, only we can relate
So will you be my Date?

11/23/2014

As our lips met, it was my first A on a test
You were mesmerized, and my lips had you hypnotized
I met your gazes and stared deeply into your eyes

Our souls connected and there was a
burning desire to keep it up running and effective...

Staring at the time

Letting days go by
We impatiently wait till the day
when we will finally meet again

A few months feels like almost 7 years,
but still, the emotion 'n love is beyond real
So, I write you this letter,

and seal it with a kiss, forever my
One and Only Paki, you are truly Missed!

2:51AM

11/23/2014

I don't understand how my life became so screwed
I crossed a line and now it's time I get back Too

Get back to where I feel from,
no I ain't Drake, but I like his whole album

Back to me, my mind is all over the place lately
I can't seem to find one simple thing to
keep my mind on track 'n my heart at peace

I do my best to rely on God,
but not just when I'm in need
He knows my heart as well as my destiny!
I just wish he'd guide me 'n make me happy
I'm on this road, and it won't lead home

Just awaiting my journey while staring at my feet,
'n they began to look dirty
A tap on the shoulder, my good Angel,
saying the Devil couldn't hold me

I know I'll rise to the occasion,
I just don't know when my feet will start moving.

11/24/2014

I have this person I miss
It hurts me when we don't speak.
Our connection was so rare, but don't get mislead,
it was definitely there!
I just wish I could see you one more time

Talk to you, sit, stare, and reminisce on old times...
That happened so quickly, 'n vanished like a mystery
I wonder if you miss me. My touch, my scent,
my laugh, my hugs, my lips, my love...

I don't know what it was,
but every time we're together,

It's perfect; like a hand 'n a rubber glove
Thinking of you at 2:15AM remembering your touch,
your kiss, your lick;

Damn near makes my body flinch!
I just miss you, so this is how I vent!
No need to reply...

Just think of this as our last Kiss
I L O V E You & Hopefully you don't forget!

2:18AM

Chapter 5

11/27/2014

So, I Love you. Am I wrong for loving?
Do you not want me too?

I'm falling in love, but you're falling too
Is that so wrong to want to be happy with you?
When I look in your eyes, I see a beautiful you

Someone so selfless whom I happen to be attracted to!
A person who is scared to love, scared to be loved,

All because of a past that will always
be a part of his life and future

I see how much you care about me
I don't see a Christian Paki, I see you roz Shaheen!!!

The man who I just happen to like and love
Tell me if I'm wrong and you don't want
there to be a you and me

I'll be hurt, but eventually I'll find peace
You can't please everybody,

but you don't have to worry about me,
I just want you to be Happy! You deserve it,

Baby

11:23AM

11/30/2014

You don't understand that you're
constantly on my mind
I can't be happy with you because
you don't want me

You miss me 'n say you love me,
but you're only being selfish because
I can't be happy knowing
that you still love me

You interfere with what
I think
I want because
I know you are what I want

1:38PM

11/30/2014

I get sad at the thought of night seeing you
Or turning around to lay on your chest in the dark
Waking up in the morning to your car,
'n horn waiting with ya arms wide open,
'n eyes shinning and smile hiding...

I get sad at the thought of you not being around
I love you now, and I want the best for you
no matter if I'm apart or not
I just wanna make you feel good
I need an extra day on the weekend

Extra hr on the clock
Just to show you how beautiful you are!

You don't know how much you mean to me

An extra month to the year, an extra holiday
just to kiss you all over your face
You're so good to me!!
You've been so good to me.

12/01/2014

What we shared was magical,
memorable, unforgettable...
For me at least! I'm trying to shake this feeling;
I don't want to, but I have too!

You were different, I was hesitant.
We both delivered and ended up happy,
all things considered

You held me how I wanted to be held
You grabbed me 'n ways that only you know

You trick me every time with those loving eyes,
heart shaped lips,
Cream toned hands that I used to hold;
that voice so calm and inviting,
Those arms that just make me feel whole.

The love I have for you is Unconditional,
no matter what the toll is
The love I have for you is old, but

somehow still has this hold;
I can't seem to shake you off heartbreak, or not.
I apologize for ever hurting you,
but now our love must continue,

45

or forever be through

I can't hang onto just a Thought of wanting you,
I must let go in order to become complete!
Letting go of my heart not missing a beat

12/10/2014

I found a man that loves me
I know, I'm Lucky! Things are difficult,
but in God we're both trusting

I don't want to mess things up, push him away,
or continuously back up
I have to get my heart on the same track

as my mind because
I wouldn't have it any other way, 'n
I would be really sad if you weren't mine

1:28PM

12/11/2014

Is there a limit to how many
Tears are spent on one person?
I'm siting here studying for my finals,
a song comes on, and you come to mind

A moment 'n time that can never be rewound,
but I keep replaying
You and Me in my mind,
I can honestly say,
I just wish we had more time

Everything that we were, all of the plans we made,
Left the day you went to PA
No if's and's or but's,
it just was simply not meant to be

But I thank you for teaching,
but I also think I hate you for ruining such a good song
With our Happy but short-lived moment that

I feel caressing my every curve every beat 'n
bump makes my leg shake
And my head begins to spin

Onto the next track, and I gasp for air, yeah,
I'm sure you remember that
It was you hitting my spot
from the Side, Front, and Back

No need to send this, I know you won't reply back.
Just had to get it off my chest since
my tears dropped each second of each song.
An album that I'll no longer listen to
without having flash backs of you.

I chose YOU over so many other people,
even my happiness
But I think it's time I choose me!
I love you with my whole heart,
But it's time I leave

1:29PM

12/24/2014

"People hate because they are taught to hate,
But they can be taught to love

47

For love comes more naturally".
-Nelson Mandela

12/29/2014

Headache and Heartache
One in the same when you allow yourself
To be subjected to the constant nonsense

Whatever the pain may be,
It's time to do better and not only reject,
But also release. Release!

11:45PM

01/01/2015

I'm not with the foolery
You should've been taking ya own advice
instead of trying to school me

I believe ya feelings are true to me,
but you care too deeply to watch her just leave
You are rushing me to leave my ex alone,
but really you never wanna leave her alone

I don't wanna pressure you,
but clearly you singing two different songs
You say you love me, but you
basically telling her it's just a quick hit 'n miss

Like we're just friends, come on now,
you ain't say that when you cried to me
Or was that just you lying to me?
No worries, I'm used to it.

48

Entering a new year like an android,
a play toy,
I no longer take you seriously and
you'll be the one paying for it

Told you not to get too comfortable,
see my heart, it bends 'n breaks,
So what more can't it take

You knew that that first cut was the deepest,
And you said you were here to fix the pieces,
When really all you did was consume space and time

It was fun, I can't lie,
But when you decide to switch,
just be up front 'n tell me why
It doesn't matter, I won't cry!

You two deserve to be,
everything you thought you had in me
Not the friend, but the "wifey" you called me

Not your encourager who wanted to
build you up and make you stronger
Not a 2AM phone call,
not your angel that you secretly called on.

3:20AM

01/04/2015

I've never met someone as beautiful as you
Your spirit and soul speak volumes
I love the person that you are,
and now I can call you MINE

I smile because you're so Damn FINE

49

You say you adore me,
and the way you hold me
Ugh, just makes me want to melt

My heart is protected in that moment
and with him I am whole
We both felt it!
I never knew I could be wanted so much!

I get butterflies just at the thought of you
Like when the sun rises and sets,
the moon comes out and says,
"Peak-a-boo my love, for you will surely Bloom!"

As you are my King, our love is bound,
And I am forever drawn to you
My future love is unknowingly powerful and baby,
I can't wait to love you

8:59PM

(As I go through, read and reflect, it amazes me the type or level of love one can have for another. By wanting to please another human being so much that you openly aid and agree to every want and need. Doing everything in your power to put a smile on one another's face and keep happiness at it's place. However, I always knew and appreciated that, but what I know understand that I didn't do or listen too as I should; not just to love but to love or be loved not only at my best but my worst and vice versa. Caring for someone at their lowest point not just their best no matter whether you're at your best or not! It's different to say it, see it and actually live it.)

Chapter 6

01/07/2015

I feel secure being with you
I never have to wonder where you're at
or whether our love is true
Who knew I would be here in this position with you..?

Loving you
Wanting you
Missing you
Constantly thinking of you

I feel as though I am going to be challenged
in new ways with you As you are
Our story is not yet finished, but unwritten
So our love will last, God willing!

10:47PM

01/08/2015

So, I guess this is like our first "fight".
I don't like it, it just doesn't feel right.
I don't know what to do without submitting

I wonder what you're thinking,
do you no longer like me? Am I not your type?

I got super sad as I watched the clock.
I won't change who I am!
I'm not perfect you should know it.
I'm not apologizing for being me,

however I do love you...
I don't know what to say.

01/30/2015

I told him I loved him
I didn't lie, but I think his love will continue to grow
I want to love him and he deserves so much more,
But at the moment, my heart is not whole

My mind says stay when my heart says go!
Our happy times, make me seem as if I am whole,
But when I'm alone at night with no one to hold
My mind wanders, my heart aches, my eyes close
And then my leg begins to shake

Not from thoughts of being with you,
But the boy my young mind is used too
I don't know if I'm still in love or
caught up in what I was used to

Sooner or later, I'll have to choose
Right now, it's as if my heart and mind
are going through World War Six

Three was the first time he cheated
Four was when I was left by the phone
waiting for a knock to say I'm home
Five was when you missed it, didn't call,
didn't show just repeated "oh yeah,

I forgot, so..." It was my birthday,
and he acted as if he didn't know
I refuse to be stuck on stupid,
But damn love sucks and the sad part is that

I still miss it!

Mean while I gotta guy who does nothing
but makes me smile
So I'm convinced that I'll lie to myself
so that it'll all work out

"I love you babe," he said with a smile,
then leaned in and whispered,
"I'm in love with you till the end."

11:51PM

02/05/2015

Love doesn't give you who you want
when you want them
Love is cruel, but also kind.
Love moves in and out of time

Just when you think you're happy,
you hear live knocking,
Blowing across your windowpane

Not as bad as the pain Love brings
When it comes, it comes with great distain
That can't be concurred by time,
that's what they say
The Wounds don't fade

You just mask them with an illusion t
hat your new Love will outlast the memories,
Good times, and old pain

Love is inevitable,
Love is when your heart is overjoyed
Shortly after the butterflies, kisses,

and hugs, comes Love's way of saying,

"No more Sunny days,
it's time for you to get stuck in the rain"
(When you're cheated on physically, your Pride is hurt
Along with Feelings
But when you're cheated on mentally,
it breaks you.)

02/07/2015

I want you deep inside me
No holding back, pull me close
while you slide into me

It may be new, but baby this is intimacy
We get to go on a ride of ecstasy
You inside of me

Me on top, submitting, or letting you pound on me
My A** slapping and clapping across you
Every time you go Deep
Isn't that how you want it..?

So you can see my Arch, watch my A**, see it giggle,
And make it bounce as you go In and Out?
You wanna see my Arch..?
You wanna hear me moan..?

Work for it, while I'm dripping down my inner thigh
From your sweet kisses, to your hand touch
Damn, I miss it! Use your tongue instead of resting
I know we won't sleep, but all I want is for you to go deep

Long and Hard make me moan, make me cum,

make me think of you
In every room, you gotta work for it
Force ya tongue till it can't stop flicking across my clit
Till I Scream out How Much I WANT Ya Dick

You can go Deeper, longer, Stronger
To get started, just show up
I promise to cater to you and make sure you stay Up
I'll lick the Tip
Rub it on my Clit
Might even do a Split!
Baby we got work to do"

If you ain't sweating, you ain't hitting' it right"
I just want both of us to enjoy our Night!

3:22AM

OUR CHOICES SHOW WHAT WE VALUE.

03/22/2015

He promised me Forever...
But I wasn't sure when it would come, or if ever!
This saddened me,
but my heart had been through tougher

I realized this man was the man for me
Prayerfully a future husband to be
Tall and strong, he would hold me in his arms.
Kiss me all night long
Want me when I'm gone

Love me through the storm
Sometimes we would even write cute little Poems
But his Heart and Mind were torn
It caused him to be sad and
his spirit always kinda morned

55

Prayer and change would help for a while
but he always found himself looking down
There wasn't much more I could say besides, "Baby,
Keep your Head up, it'll be ok.
We can get through it
Just continue to pray!"

These words I spoke lasted for a while,
till one day he stumbled and again fell down
I want nothing more than to see your
smile and hear your voice,

But that void you're feeling will only
change when your circumstances begin to fade
Just remember the Sacrifice that was made
by Jesus in order for us to get here

Your storm isn't over, and baby,
remember there's only UP from here!
I love you deeply and hopefully

One day your Heart, Mind, Body and
Soul will forever and internally be healed
No matter what, I'll be standing by your side,

Even if we're both in wheel chairs
I vow to love you and never leave you!

3:59AM

03/23/2015

I'm not going to sleep because
I know you aren't And I won't rest well till
I can feel your Healed heart

My mind is restless wondering what you're doing

My heart is heavy believing your thoughts may be pure
My eyes are closed for the moment when
I feel you have lost all hope

My head is bowed down as
I mumble and whisper a special prayer
for your true heart's desire to be found
If I could, I'd wrap my arms around you and

Sit quietly with you as we begin to float
in a stream of tears happy and sad,
But eliminated of fears

On Flesh, Even when we're not chest to chest,
I can feel the uneasiness, so I don't really rest
I can see the weepiness just by your eyes
When I looked into them,
I saw a tortured 'n frightened soul

Broken, not whole
I pray for you and you're healing as a whole
I Ask God to send you Angels to
hold you up so that you don't fold!
Just hang on and press forward
Those angels won't let go

Just remember, you're not alone!
I have a few stories about being in a dark hole,
A crowded room 'n still feeling alone;
an empty space with no home,
A pill bottle or knife wound to end it all

But if I made it through, you can too
'Cause I'm nowhere as tough as you are!
ROZ, you gotta stand strong
And remember, you're NOT Alone

1:29AM

57

03/31/2015

Every time I see you,
I want you to make love to me
Every time I smell your cologne,
it reminds me of our first time

Every time you smile,
it reminds me of all our Good Times
Which is something I no longer have
It hurt then, and it hurts now!

9:36PM

04/12/2015

You can get what you want
And not want what you have

And when you get what you want,
realize it's already been had
Leave what you thought you wanted,
and still feeling all sad

3:12AM

04/14/2015

What do you do when the door shuts?
No ones around, the silence is your only sound

Your tears begin to fall like rain
What do you do when the one your with is no longer enough?

Your heart's desires are more than you can bear

You stop to think about the other person

Your heart cares, but feelings aren't really there
What do you do when you look around and you are all you have?

How can you heal and grow when you're
feeling stuck with nowhere to go?

Should you sit 'n cry, and let the darkness take over,
or close your eyes 'n wish it was all over?

8:24PM

Chapter 7

04/16/2015

Okay, so I don't really know what to say...
You're not my dude 'n still you kinda
just made my heart melt...

Not my usual style, but whenever I see you, my mind....
'n thoughts start to wander all crazy 'n wild.....

Real laidback, in the cut Yeah I like that .....
Your subtle spirit 'n cool ways pulled me in...

It wasn't day to day, but still
I stuck around 'n you stayed hip.....
I had a dream about you the other day,
and I got hot! Yeah, you hear what I say....

I want you like you want me,
but at the end of the day, we would never be....
Sexual tension when in the room;
our hearts beat like a bad condition.....

You just pull me closer and slightly
'n aggressively love me all over,
Till my leg keeps shaking....
My lor secret but we would never call
each other lovers, just a mutual understanding
between to sexual beings....

. Behind closed doors, I can just imagine
\you making me scream....
When I'm hot, you give me what I need.....

When you call, I come thru and give you the things
Your body craves and your mind needs....
I never told you, but you make me
want you more 'n more....
Yeah it's sexual, but either way,
I fucks wit Chu more 'n more...

If you were to hit me up or came
knocking at my door,
I'd answer, I'd listen, then ask you,
"Where do you want me?"

"The bed or the floor..?"
It's just what we do
No one would understand,
But Shhhhhh, we do!

12:11AM

04/16/2015

I usually just write to myself...
But I guess I'm like Drake;

I decide to share with someone else.
Hope you like. This one is titled:

"My New High"

It's something about Chu
I don't wanna scare you away or frighten you,
but damn,
I really like you

It's something about Chu...
Maybe it's the way you walk, talk and smile
Maybe it's ya personality and laidback cool style

Or maybe it's when I look into your eyes and stare,
and you never blink;
You just stay right there
With your beautiful brown eyes and
soft skin that drives me wild

Or maybe the way I picture your
hands caressing my body
As if we're intertwined or united
It's something about you

Like a first time high that I can't get through
I'm infatuated with you and all you do
Addicted to this high like the highest ride

I'm not obsessed 'n I'm not crazy,
I'm just riding this high cause it feels amazing
It's something about Chu and
I don't even know what cha name is,
I guess it's time I start turning the pages

Although things didn't work out,
I turned the pages and like that *snaps*,
You just faded
I found someone better in this chapter, someone
who would fill me with joy and laughter.
But most of all, roses

White Roses

He gave me flowers. They were Roses.
"Why aren't they RED?" I asked
He replied, "When you came into my life,
I began to see better
Red reminded me being under the weather,
no love, and just cloudy days with no cover

You came into my life and made all the rain go away"
I replied, "How sweet of you,
do you know that everything happens for a reason?
And if this works, I'll be around longer than a season."

He smiled 'n grinned, with eyes so innocent;
I just had to let him in
He was a beautiful man, and called me his queen
My silence filled the air
His Kiss was so debonair

Together we worked, 'n so we stayed right there,
With the sun shinning on my white Roses
"PURE," is what he told me

I giggled, but he began to hold me
2 months, and this man already knows me
A white rose to represent our secret Love!

10:04PM

04/16/2015

Yeah, I was in love once
We were all in love right..?
You know the feeling

The itching, the cringing,
the tears, and the heartache?
Makes you feel like you're on a pipe or syringe,
and you're in bad need of an update
But I was in love, right?

We were all in love, right..?
You know, the kinda love
that had you up in the morning till 6AM
I had at 8AM, but YOU, you alone were my filler and

I couldn't get enough

I wanted to be by your side,
ride shotgun when you drive
Wipe your tears, help you eliminate
all fears, be your get away
Yeah, I was in love once,
but we were all in love, right?

When you can barely think straight
Wondering what they're doing.
Should you call, do you think
he/she is still Up—This late..?
Or when your calls 'n text go
unanswered and your mind freaks out

Like (worry) oooh-man I hope I get a answer!
Outside Ya House waiting in the car like, you good..?
Just checking 'cause you know
I called, but I didn't get an answer

But we've all been in love right?
That passionate feeling we feel
if we were to hit the blunt just right..?
(Pause)

It'll ease ya mind, comfort you, hold you tight.
Is it still love when you get struck down..?
And you're forced to wear sunglasses now
Is it love when you can no longer trust,
But jump at the sound or thought of being touched.

Is it love when you hold my hand in the ER 'n
Help me come up with a Lie like
the reason for my broken ribs,
Or reoccurring scars?
Love, Nah.

Love?

Huh, I guess you never thought of the love
I craved for you
The pain that made me stay with you
The love that we're all addicted to
The love that makes me a Fiend too!

What I thought was love,
I no longer have to give to you!
But I was in love once, yeah,
we were all in love once...Right?

But don't let that love tear you down
And have you crying in the
darkness without a sound
Love shouldn't hurt, it should be carefree,
make you think, feel 'n believe in anything

So don't fall in love with that crack pipe or
that tap-tap, just let me get another hit, right!
Don't fall for the thugs, gangsters,
'n pretty boys who tell you lies

Fellas, don't always believe these girls, so quick,
In ease to take their skirts off
when really they just need a hug,
Or the gold diggers that are hiding
behind daddy issues

Yeah, don't fall in love with the high of being in love
'Cause if it's real, you shouldn't have to feel hurt
Or wanna disappear behind those lies

10:11PM

04/26/2015

I can think of a few things
Yeah, I can let you do some things

Starting with ya hands wrapped around me,
Until they lift me up and place me down
where you want me

Or should I say, where I wanna be.
I can imagine your tongue all over me
With ya sweet chocolate lips that
I'm sure I'm gonna miss

I'll give you details in HD as long as you
plan to deliver what I need
Whether it's Face Time or a Quickie,
I'm planning on getting all that you have to give me!
Take my clothes off, I'll take your shirt off

Slowly kissing and teasing you,
but you're a man, so it excites 'n aggravates you
I'll stop, no need to ruin the mood
Remove your pants, climb on top of you
But don't rush, I'm already dripping wet for you

But now it's your turn to taste me too!
You was frontin' for a while,
But I won't hold that against you
Yeah, you talk a lot of shit,
But once you put them lips against my clit,
that's me shutting you up like if
I was to get on my knees and suck ya dick...

You know how you love that shit

At the end of the day,
You always back it up with your Big Dick,
But you know this, I told you before you
"Have a Nice Penis"

11:31AM

04/29/2015

Laying here. Daydreaming of you pulling on my Hair
Your hands running up and down my body
Your arm around my throat while
I embrace your deep strokes!

Out and in, you love to watch my body cringe,
As you lean down grab hold of my waist and thrust down
I seem to let out a sound,
a sweet sexual sensual moan sound

There's just this little bit about you that makes me
Want you inside and around me now
You roll me over now you on top

Staring me in my eyes making
your dick hard n my heart throb,
My legs shake and faces I begin to make

I bite my lip and you grab hold of my titties;
We ain't making love but this is some good-good and
We prolly both been missing it

3:19PM

06/01/2015

If I give you my all, I know I won't fall
But I'm just scared

I know you may wonder if
my heart 'n head is all in

But as long as you need me,
I will do my best to be there
I promised to always be honest with you,
so that's what I'll do

I'd be lying if I said I weren't over my ex, 'n
I hate the fact that you're giving me
your all and my performance is less

I don't care to see or speak to him, and
I understand your position completely,
But I'm not giving up on us—on me
On our love continuing to grow 'n blossom
beautifully It scares me that I could've

9:00PM

06/04/2015

I just wanna get my mind off of things
Like a needle in a hay stack,
lost in between an in between
And lately, it seems you, you,
'n you only wanna get in between

Crawl deep in between my thighs 'n things
But don't stick around to wipe my eyes if I cry you see
You never really wanted to know me.

Just become a part of me Physically Emotionally
Because now you see we're Soul Tied
And ain't no breaking that bond

So, before you go off 'n run off'

68

n jack off, up 'n ya new little hunny, you see,
I'ma need you to realize a few things. Like:

1. I am a Black Queen
2. I am beautiful
3. I just realized I really DON'T need you

So, don't try to fill my head with lies
before you kiss my inner thigh or
Caress my face 'n tell me how sweet
I smell 'n taste.
Just wait...

Instead of going In between my breasts 'n things,
I think you should learn to spell 'n speak correctly,
So that when you're beaten down or yelled at,

You can lash out, fight back, and speak up,
Don't hold back, correctly

Politically correct, legitimately in check,
demanding Respect
And leaving behind more than what was left!

1:18AM

06/05/2015

The hours are constantly fading with you
Our love continues to Blossom 'n bloom

Our hearts beat in sync and in tune
Wherever your are, will remain my home

12:48AM

06/05/2015

I'm an outsider here. I'm an outsider there
It just seems like I don't fit in anywhere!
My wish isn't to fit in,

But simply stay strong while my Heavenly
Father arranges a few things
In a kingdom fit for a Queen

I do not wish to conform,
but I will however bend and transform
Like a caterpillar, to it's beautiful Butterfly form

I won't stay the same,
and the sight may be strange to
those in the middle of a storm

I wish no one harm,
but to go to meet Jesus with open arms

8:32PM

Chapter 8

06/07/2015

I love how in love you are with me
I cry tears of joy just knowing you're there for me
I never once took you for granted,
but thanked god for sending me such a great man!

You are my light, inside and out
When I met you, I knew
I would want my son to look, act, and behave as you do
I'm not just in love with you,
I'm secretly crazy about you

I'll cherish every kiss
Every hug, every stare into your beautiful brown eyes
It was just something about "dem eyes though"

They pulled me in with such genuine innocence
It made me never want to let go
You said I "made your day,"
Well I apologize in advance for
crushing your hopes, our dreams, and your soul

I'll pray for God to bring us back together,
but for right now,
I just don't know

You're the perfect man,
hopefully my future self's perfect Husband!
Take care of yourself, and please, don't hate me

4:22PM

06/21/2015

This man Loves everything about me
And it's so crazy, I feel so lazy,
so undeserving of your love, it's beyond Amazing
I can look in your eyes 'n see your telling the truth
I can feel you pledge your allegiance in a simple hug
I can hear your truth in every "I want you."

I believe everything you say, but still,
that's not why I stay
I'm fighting for a future.
We're fighting to love 'n pull through
You're fighting for my heart and
it's in Awe of you

12:09AM

06/27/2015

This is for now, not forever
Remember, our love can storm the weather

Just as sure as the sun will shine
Baby, in the end, you're mine

2:52AM

07/10/2015

I LOVE YOU!!!!
Soooo much

Can't wait to give you my last name
Can't wait to marry you

Can't wait to live with you

Can't wait to sleep with you and wake up to you
Can't wait to come home to you!
I love you sooooo freakin' much!
Don't ever leave me

We gon fight every fight together
No matter what it is
We will fuss and argue!
But we will get through it

Our love will grow stronger as we go
through difficult times
But we shall never give up on us no matter
what it isDon't ever hide, lie,
cheat, put me down in any kind of way

A nigga keep pushing it, I need to know
A nigga trying to get to you flirting, I need to know!
All I ask is for your love and loyalty

Anybody coming for you,
they coming for me too! It's just me and you
So tell these niggas to face it cuz
God gave me you so why the fuck would I replace it!?

I will always put you first.
And one day we will be official,
no more hiding from people
No more of what others feel about us being together
No more of what others think or what they got to say!

We will live our life future for us
and our future beautiful kids you will give me
A happy married life with a happy

and everlasting happiness with our own family
That we will bring forth
I love you more than you can ever think baby!

2:32PM

08/09/2015

With you I have a love to last a lifetime
With you, I have a love so divine

With you, I love eternally and extraordinarily
With you, I have found my heart's beat
My smile is now complete

You are the wind beneath my wings
With you, I will spend my life.
With you, GOD sent me a blessing so true

With you, I love wholeheartedly
With you, I am complete and so much more

You are my beginning and end
You are my night and day
You are God sent

You are one of the best things to
ever happen to me
And with this short poem,
you make me feel Complete!

5:12PM

08/23/2015

Beauty and grace Angel,
we are all deeply saddened since you left this place

Angel, our sweet Angel

She always put a smile on your face
And on August 13th, she bowed out and
left this earth with such joy and grace

As each and every year fills this place,
we wish to just touch 'n
feel your precious face
In our hearts we now ache.
Wishing you were here to comfort us and...

4:20pm

08/28/2015

You're not just an Angel, but a jack of All trades
Loving, caring, and most of all,
kept a smile on your face

My love, my Heart, the feeling
I have for you will never escape
Forever an angel in the sky,

but a lion at heart
I admire how hard you fought
and each and every one of us love you for it

As we lay you to rest on this day
we find peace in knowing
That you are floating above in heaven's skies

Without a care in the world,
no bills to calculate 'n multiply,
No kidney treatment to tire you out,

but joy and happiness

Filled with granny's Hugs and laughter
If only you knew how much

I'm going to miss you in this next chapter
I promise to write you everyday, and if I don't,
I'll just look up and smile at the end of everyday...

Just knowing you're only a few miles
away and awaiting me at heaven's gate
So, know that I love you and will do my best
so that mama will never have to struggle
This isn't good bye, just a see you next time!

Always and forever my angel in the sky...
Life isn't about your Final moments
It's about the moments that lead up to them

10:43AM

09/01/2015

For someone to know my passion is to know me
To truly understand my heart's
desires and help me get to where
I want to be

You are and will always be the man for me
To hold my hand, comfort,
and support me in my time of need

10:51AM

09/28/2015

My letter to you

It's clear that I love you

76

I can visibly see the pain that you're going through
I don't know the hurt your heart feels,

But my mind 'n body also understands that,
I too lost an angel.
However,

She was so dear to you! My heart aches just knowing
That I can't help you escape your never ending heartbreak
Just know that GOD's plan is never a mistake
I can visibly see that you want to be alone

Simply because you're feeling lost with no home
It saddens me because I know your worth
I feel you're hurt every time
I close my eyes and picture
our Angel leaving this earth

I smile knowing that she won't ever
have to endure anymore hurt
I can visibly see you wanting and
wishing to be invisible, but trust in God,

He will pull you through the hardest of times
Know that I love you and I may not be your twin,
But just as you were with her,
I will be with you until the very end!

10:24PM

09/v31/2015

I fucking hate you right now
I feel like shit! Like, the person
I was or am is in between 2 different ships

Maybe your sister was right,

77

"I'm just another black bitch,"
And they'll be another and another '

Cause cars clothes and money won't make me stay
Your controlling aggressive ways will
only continue to push me away,

And I'm a black queen
Not just someone who stays home,
bend over backwards and wash, cook, and clean

You say you want a black girl,
but do you really know what that means!?

Independent
Smart
Feisty
Cook
Clean
But also has her own life to lead.

My last dude sheltered me,
but you you just want to put a shell around me.
Make me your own personal little Barbie doll.
Cook, clean, walk, speak, and never yell AT all!

I packed a bag just the other day
I packed a bag, and wanted to run away
I should've never taken your card,
the love you Gave me was just way to hard!

6:11PM

02/28/2016

End of May it is!!!

78

I could write a book of all of my fantasies
All my fantasies that don't involve you

My fantasies that make even
dominatrices turn blue

My fantasy, just thinking about it with you
Makes my knees shake with
a puddle of my juices overcoming you

3:07PM

05/30/2016

It started with a text
Yeah, that's right, I said it, a text
And then came along the sex

But before the sex,
he had already passed the test

And then next there was his smile,
his love, they way
I felt when he looked at me,
the comfort I felt in his arms
He was sent here for me
A man of God truly

Not perfect, but more than worth it
Thinking this would just be a season or fling thing,
But I see now you were sent to me with a purpose

1:21AM

Chapter 9

07/05/2016

If I could fill a blank page with all
my subliminal and critical,
My message would bring about a new ice age

In this world it's so cold but but
I hope my words will remain embedded

In your brain like a match to a flame;
catch on 'n spread the word like wild fire,
I'm saying this so we all can stay united

We gotta stop fighting one another
Help each other ignite a spark that
our future children and

Grandchildren will be proud to carry our name!
Make a difference is what I'm saying

10:14PM

07/06/2016

Deep
You defined LOVE for me

It's like every breath came naturally,
every heart beat chased after you
You are my writing muse

Sometimes, I HATE you because my

80

heart is still confused
I don't mean to be rude,
but I don't know what else to do
My MIND is haunted by you

My thoughts are finally starting to get rid of you
You don't understand how much
I LOVE you

But this is just how I vent since
I lost you and you were my Best friend too.
Sad, but true

I'll be fine just learning to LIVE without you!
My heart still HURTS and that's
why I can't speak to you

So, shoutout to you 'n the Missus,
either way to me, they'll all be some Bitches!!
But don't mind me, just letting out my Bitterness
You really fucked me over

I feel like your actions and Heart grew a bit colder
Along with the distance 'n separation you find stuff
In your new life to use as your clinical medication
(Not literally) I just hope you don't lose your grip
Stay focused, you can manage it

I'm just rambling on
No need to reply or read,
I'm just going through my feelings, you know me

Unfortunately!
I would send you the rest but that would be like sending you a short
novel

Of what it feels like to be my

HEART everyday Anyway
Hope you have a great life
filled with much success

07/06/2016

Sexual Tension.
I want you!

The attraction I have to you is no longer new,
but very unusual
You're my First, my Last,
and My only

I want you whether you believe it's true or not
I want you!

I day dream about being with you
I miss your company, smile,
and conversation that had us up till 2AM

But sleep didn't matter, as long as
we were together
I dream about your touch,
even when I'm Horny and want to F**

Just the other day I wanted your taste.
To feel your lips and hold your waist

My tongue gently and erotically
stroking your beautifully shaved kitty
While your inner thigh slightly begins to shake,

I then speed up my tongue and

82

watch as your heart races and we start an Earthquake
My lips all over your beautiful brown skin.
I want you!

If I don't ever get to have you in life,
just let me Hold, you one night

I want you 'n I promise to keep up while
I keep you up from night to day
From the morning Sun to the Night shade
Baby, I just wanna love you
intimately and physically
I want you. This is all true!

I was gonna keep these thoughts hidden,
but I figured why not make you smile
Maybe even give you a thought or

You left an impression
Whether or not the feeling is mutual,
I just felt like writing
Especially since I'm HORNY too!
Love you Z boo!

8:55PM

07/06/2016

Mistake
Wondering if I made a mistake..?

At the end of the day, my choice 'n
choices will leave someone undone
More than one heart stung

Wondering if I made a mistake maybe
I shouldn't have looked into the beautiful brown eyes

Maybe I should have been okay with the lies
But that's all in the past now,

All I have is broken glass in the
tiniest parts of my throat that cut like a knife
when he could've, should've,
would've removed them to hear me laugh

But now, I'm here wondering if I made a mistake
Like damn maybe I just shouldn't date
But your smile so appealing, your laugh so sweet,
and your hands so comforting
But as I sit 'n look through the glass you see,
that other girl is hurting
That other girl is worried

That other girl is hungry, for something new,
For something real, for something further
than the new Michael Kors bag,

$50,000 credit limit, and luxury gifts
you've been giving.
You say I deserve them because I'm a queen,
but when I look at you,
Your actions scream "my little prize thing"

Wondering if I made a mistake
because everybody doesn't seem to be smiling,
And even tho my lips are silent,
my thoughts aren't one sided,

My clouded judgment, yeah, it speaks volumes, but
As I lay in your arms wanting you to keep me warm

Maybe you should've just weathered the storm
Rather than getting involved with your aura
Yeah, you 'n me were soul tied 'n

I know about another 3 who has had a part of me,
And now I'm trying to break free!

But I'm just here wondering if maybe I made a mistake
Was I suppose to invite you over?
Did God intend for me to cry on your shoulder?
Cause our love seems to be poison;
slowly spreading to the living
Our families not seeing our true intentions

At the end of the day, only one truly knows your fate
But still wondering, did I do right
or should I regret this lifelong mistake?

I'm tryna spit some truth
I don't have nobody to tell or anybody who cares

I just need another bottle so
I can go into details
I'll spare you the boring details 'n
get right down to the tea now
I use to be suicidal

Yeah, my ex that bum ass nigga he's my idol
Gave him the world 'n shitted on me
like Jordan in high school
But never mind that fool

My life was shaken and
I needed some new news,
some new food

9:02PM

07/28/2016

Black deaths are sad

85

Yeah, I said it, black deaths
Because we are the ones that get overlooked;
My people are the ones that are left
lying dead bleeding out crying out yelling for help!

Black deaths are sad, but then again,
so is the death of losing a loved one or a friend
They constantly televise it so
that they can start an uprising and
you start a hell fire

Or the continuous situation of a violent riot.
Don't you see?
The white man, the trigger puller,
the capital hill, the final voter,

The deal closer is hiding in the dark playing
puppet master controlling your shoulders
The police, the government, the society, the republicans,
They are the antagonists to the story which is your life
And the writing which isn't right;
and the ink that has dried over night

Life just don't seem right.
Ignore the hype,
A hashtag and repost won't
bring our brothers 'n sisters back to life

We must stand together, open our eyes and
realize the American disguise
Hiding behind a mask of never ending lies

Let's hold off the inevitable because
our black men are more than credible
Don't defame their name with lies and hypocrisy
The truth used to be in the pudding,
but evil wears a mask you see

Black deaths are sad and
it's even sadder when they're across every news feed
Enraging the inside of you and me

Displayed on TV 'n computer screens,
taken far too early, but never resting
entirely rolling over in the grave seeing
these guilty men walk away

The justice system full of mistakes,
and now I'm here crying out
for my people to hear Black deaths are sad, but unless

We come together stick together
it could be you or me
In order to make a difference,
we must think different
Pray to your God or mine,

it's time for a higher power to reign,
It doesn't start with Trump or Hilary

Hold onto your dignity,
but keep in mind your ability
Don't feed into negativity

2:42AM

07/31/2016

No one knows the real me
No one knows I write, or my insecurities

No one knows I have this gift—
this desire burning deep inside me
No one knows me

11:45PM

09/07/2016

How can you see the light when
you're constantly surrounded by darkness?
Drawn to the wrath of
My heart aches

My heart aches because
I can't put a smile on my grandmother's face
My heart aches and all I keep hearing is,
"don't worry, it's not your place,"

As God is my witness my heart and
mind bear the weight
For my true heart's intent.
I want nothing more than to help
and see others soar

With smiling faces and hearts so warm
My heart aches more than the pain
in my side from working two
doubles staying up late

My heart aches, but not because
I work endlessly or sweat blood and tears
But my heart aches because
I feel like I'm failing my family and...

11:47PM

Part I

"My Secret Side"

02/11/2017

Me speaking is me releasing
I love
I hate
I'm human
I made a mistake
Growing every day

The look on your face, the silence inside open space,
The wounds I clearly created,
the damage that you can't seem to shake
I love you.

And you love me
We're sisters, so it's what God intended for us to be
You walking away,
or me putting those tears on your face
I've become a disgrace

I never intended but now all I wanna do is wipe them away
Share a shoulder, be your blanket when you're colder
Find my only true Best friend 'n Console her

I messed up big 'n I know it
I just hope you 'n God allow me to resew it
Stitch it up 'n repair it with more
than a few dollars 'n some family alliances
I want it to be better, but I'm not sure you do...

I don't want you up stressed 'n crying in the middle
Of the night without me there to comfort you
Give me your problems 'n

I'll gladly lighten it your load, you feeling alone
I pray God heals both you 'n
I and we have a new Sister Hold!

I'm not giving up 'n I'm not letting go
So the next time you walk in a room 'n don't speak,
I'll come sit on your lap 'n tell you all that you mean to me
I love you 'n you're still my

One and Only Everything,
Call on me whenever you need!
The secret is out, I want everyone to see
what you mean to me

4:45PM

Part II
"My Secret Side"

I feel empty
Like there's a closed door
I'm trying to get through and a
darkness that's so filling

My mind wandering and heart racing
bringing tears to my eyes and
I feel like I can't take it

Don't wanna be caged in,
lord help me don't let the devil take me!
I have to fight, hold on, and kick to make it

But honestly I can say,
I'm feeling caged in empty, scared and alone
But with no one around to hold,
I drop to my knees

Fold my hands 'n begin to pray a prayer 'n
call out "Oh God, just Help me!"

I wonder if he hears my cries,
I believe he does because he saved my from a fight 'n
The battle of my life against cancer and I WON
Only GOD can do that

Take me from the natural and turn
my situation to supernatural,
And it's all for his glory you see

But now I feel as tho I'm on the run, trying to get away,
Run from myself, get away 'n be free,
or just run to some help

Just away from the Empty, Cold,
Sad, Scared, Mess, And Loneliness

So, I call out unto God and I have
FAITH that he will answer 'n supply my every need
GOD, my lord, 'n Jesus Christ, he is ALL I need!

4:56PM

Part III

"My Secret Side"

Who knew my secret side?
Who knew that when I put pen to paper I feel alive?
My secret side, who knew God was alive?
(Who knew Jesus himself cared enough?)

Constantly moving in silence when you think
you're forgotten
His timing is late, but always great
Maybe he was a brother trying to make his court date

Don't doubt his power,
don't stray from your faithful father
With God, his only secret is his great escape

My secret side
I wonder at night will I be resurrected if I died
No tears to cry, I just sit and
wait patiently by the kings right side
Preparing for that day

That day of judgment when
I finally get to reach, get to breathe,
get to see his presence

My secret side, I'm kinda scared to die
Will I meet my guardian angel, will
I have wings to fly, will my house be pleasing to the Lord?

Good measure and approval is what
I'm looking for

My secret side
I pray to God I don't have to hide
I beg of him like a thief in the night,
let my works be mighty in your sight

Let me not fail you, denying you
three times before the rooster even crows
Calling out in the middle of the night
You are my Shining light

Let me leave this dream that we may call life,
and live in eternity with no sin in sight
Who knew my secret side..?
Who knew that when I found Jesus and
accepted him as lord of my life,
I would still have to fight?

Who knew that that last stripe was taken for me?

For you to even think of creating me
Like one grain of a sand in the sea
My secret side

I hope it's clear for all to see
I serve the one and only living God
And he is who I chose to be

12:37AM (July 17)

02/11/2017

How is it that a female is able to
withstand numerous attacks on her Heart?

One unintentional comforting night turns a male that
One male that you think you could
spend your life brings their world
crashing down at the speed of light

Of course you didn't mean it,
But there was this other guy who
just comforted you 'n made you feel alright
Not in spite, but a Male can't stand the sight

Or even hear the words you
speak to him in plain sight
I just wanna know why we are,
females held to a higher standard

After undergoing almost drowning with hurt,
pain, sorrow, and most of all, heartache
But a male, the one who plays the role of a Man,

But yet continuously breaks down a

woman by cheating, Being a dog, Calling her a hoe,
Bringing home a child and a maternity note,

Walking out so many times 'n
expect the love to remain the same,
While you appear to still be whole

The pain of the two can't be controlled all because of
Eve and an uneasy urge that she
actually should've never known nor conceived

As she reached for that forbidden fruit,
Adam began to turn in his sleep,
Having dreams he could've never even thought of
When they first met in the field or street

When she was naked, he could not see
But as Eve grew closer to a lie, as she reached for the fruit,
Her true desires changed from honey to gold
Wanting what she never knew,
craving sin and turning away from the truth

Adam then lusted for her amongst
others he had never even known
Sleeping so peacefully as God told
So, from here on out, we're left to blame,
being made from a man's Rib cage,

His faults 'n mistakes came
from the temptation that Eve introduced to thee
Don't let the devil disguise you as
he reveals himself as the Prince of Peace

We may not be naked to what the eye can see,
But our Hearts are as naked and embarrassed as can be
No hiding from Love

Fruit. Clothes Or the Tree
Present your self to God with All Humility!

5:02PM

Chapter 10

03/13/2017

My vow to you.
I vow to love you

Not just because you're handsome,
with beautiful brown eyes
Or because you never tell me lies

Or because you're always there to
wipe the tears from my eyes if I should ever cry
I vow to love you

Because you deserve the love you give me
Your beautiful energy and
kindred spirit deserves love endlessly
I'll take your heart and continue to heal it

I vow to love you because
I know it's God's plan for us to love one another,
unconditionally
I vow to love you, just as roz is to a
King and Jasmine is a Flower's sea
I vow to love you and take you as my King

I loving you was me falling for you
I falling for you was me walking in God's plan
Like he is the head

Center and my whole
But his plan had me sold

11:38AM

07/20/2017

It's me jumping off the ledge it's
me trying to hold onto my head
Trying to forget the things he said!

2:17AM

07/27/2017

I don't know if you know,
but I write poetry from time to time
I'm like a young modern day Drake
with breasts and a prettier face

It's just my thoughts, things
I don't usually share with anyone else
Something to pass the time,
I usually just write when I'm sad or angry
I'm a little bit of both with a whole lot of other stuff...

You make my body feel things I haven't felt in a while
You make me think in ways that makes my body talk
Any who, instead of writing and
demonstrating my hurt and anger,

I decided to turn it into a sexual expression
of my sensual encounter
From loneliness to desire,
this time I'm more descriptive
Okay, so here it goes. It starts like this...

My body and Mind seems to crave you
Your thick Man, an extension of
you growing hard and stronger inside me

97

Not too poetic, just straight to the point

No stalling, we both know what we want
Filling up my walls bringing, my juices down,
Making my legs and knees shake,
the vibration of you on me,

And me on you cause my whole body to quake for you
And all the sexual pleasure you bring too!

My body and Mind seem to crave you
because you paid attention to me
You wanted to please me

You explored my body like it was a grand prize or treasure
My exotic thoughts just continue to grow
Having flash backs of me and you

Picturing us in a fantasy world that's
nonstop, exhilarating, mind blowing sex
My Body and Mind seem to crave you
because you actually called me back
You made the effort to stay around

Even if it was only to get ya Dick wet and licked
We both gained some as soon as sun the sun rose
No love or staying in our feelings

I guess there should be less calls 'n texts between us
Which will only drive us crazy in the beginning
Who knows, maybe even create
a new spark with the sex

Distance makes the heart grow fonder they say...
Well distance makes me fuck you harder each day
It's just good company and our
bodies are what we're exploring

Reaching higher heights with me on top and
you insideYour facial expressions give me
slight pleasure as if I'm your morning coffee
Your wake and bake to get you started

Eat me
Drink me
Please me
Tease me

My mind and body craving you is like me cursing you
Enticing you with all the sexual tricks I do
Making you Text back like "yeah shorty,

I want that" or a simple "good morning beautiful"
Yeah, you just say all the things
I've been missing in the distance

You act as if you want me just as much as your other man stands to
attention when
I come around or lick you down

No biggie, I like what were doing
How you make me feel
How you kiss, touch, 'n hold me.
Every time we kick it, your soft sexy lips on mine

From my lips to my neck
No leaving marks or a scratch
That's my job, slowly flowing down to caress
rub, lick, and suck on my breasts now

Your lips are like ecstasy sweet, soft, and so sexy
After you lick me down, constantly telling me you want me
Or I'm on your mind (like I shouldn't be)
Either way, you be feeling me like I'm feeling you

And we both agreed to keep our cool, so
I hope my body and Mind get on track with the plan
Instead of moving to a beat of its own

I know you may think this is way
too long or maybe you won't

Perhaps you'll be intrigued and it'll turn you on
It's a positive way of how I'm choosing to deflect
Thinking of how you move when you're inside me
Or the fact that I imagine it being just like that
Fitting so perfectly inside me

Right after I spit on it and sit on it
You grab me and make me ride to our own beat
All with me slow grinding so you

feel everything inside me winding
I know how you like when I fuck you back
We're slowly becoming attached

With every stroke kiss lick and flash back
My naughty yet poetic mind wanders from time to time
And thinks that it's been way too long...

Since you grabbed my ass
Kissed me, smiled and asked why I'm so good to you
Because you fuck me how I want you to

Who knew I like that shit?
Like when you choke me and pull me deeper
Or smack my ass

Waiting on you to hit it from the back,
While I do that thing you like to
make you think you're on vacation
Inside me all day and night

No rush, I plan on keeping this up as long as you let me
4 years and you still wanted me
No stalling just counting
down until the next visit

You have a really nice penis,
and I'm writing this because I miss it!

5:58AM

07/31/2017

I ain't even charge you,
I let you hit for free, now you be hitting me
hittin' me like why you so good to me

We ain't goin' steady, we just be fuckin' 'round
Keep all ya feelings and emotions somewhere else,
they don't belong 'round

This is my note to self 'cause I really miss the kid
Knowing that I'm catching feelings,
I gotta put them things to bed

You dick me down and then you lay me down
Staring into my eyes before it goes down

I gotta shake this feeling 'cause the
position I'm in is more than hectic,

I don't want to pull you under while I'm going down
But I honestly enjoy having you around
I don't mean to send you mixed signals, but
I'm feeling you and I feel like I shouldn't

You show me attention and affection, 'n

101

That's something I've been missing
You told me to keep it a stack,

so we both be keeping our word with that
I don't want you to fall for me,
I'm something like a day time drug;

I get you hooked 'n
leave you wanting more when
you ain't got no money

I fucked you silly 'n left you running
home to ya mommy
I just hope you don't hate me
No matter how we end,

I fucks with you like Wonder
Woman and DC comics

4:46PM

August 1, 2017

Sitting here 707 President Street
11:51PM on July 12th or 13th, 2017,

62 days after my husband told me
he cheated on me
Wishing I was pregnant

With a horrible gut feeling
Because I want to do this right

Not giving into a weak moment of
weakness wanting me to come spend the night
But instead, I take FLIGHT

On to new heights, this all started
as me releasing my thoughts,
Not a poem or a rap or someone's piece of art

But this is all coming from the heart
With 5 minutes to spare before I walk 'n get to work,
I have to write down this hurt
Of abandonment, broken, and torn down to dirt
It really hurts

I want to be pregnant, feel a life inside of me
Feel a love that's never felt,
a hug that can just make you melt

A beautiful breathtaking boy or girl
That I call mine and protect in this cold world
Not to keep my husband, but to fill a void,
to complete me and
Be proud of me when I soar

I wouldn't tell him
Not meaning to rob him of his choice
But not making him stay either without feeling forced

No. 'Cause me 'n my baby would be good
Leave him and stay pure!

Not forcing it in him to be a husband,
father, or stay
But man enough to accept it anyway

I'm just sitting here
Putting my faith in God

To put pen to paper 'n delete and
block all those other guys!
I will NOT cheat, I will not let his actions

dictate mine

I will stand firm on my faith and
Love on my GOD
Devil, you can't have me

Temptation may be hard, but my
spirit man will help me fight and guard my heart
So, to the little person that will one
day grow and be made of me

You will not be a mistake
God will bless you and me
I will love you eternally

I want you because I know you'll love me
Sincerely your Future mom, until we meet!
12:03AM
12:05AM

No I won't do it on purpose, that's not right in my eyes, but
I will wait and pray for
God to continue to make things right!

12:05AM
(numbers are important; or they can be)

12:46AM

08/09/2017

He not a dope boy, an only smoke boy,
get a drink or two

He make me fiend like
I'm on some coke boy
He put in work boy

Like, is you woke boy?
But he can be a gentleman,
he let me use his face as my surfboard

He wipe my mouth when we finish
I say my grace and he deliver
He beat it up like we serving...

6:54PM

August 21, 2017

My world's not falling apart,
it's falling into place

When I'm on my knees n
answers seem so far away

9:46PM

10/18/2017

What do I think of you..?
I never answered your question
You're something like the Sun & the Moon

At certain parts of the day or night,
you allow me to see all of you
I could've just written you a list or called you back,
but what fun is that?

So, I decided to put it in the form of a
poetic rap or a haiku using more than
7–17 lines and a rhyme filled with similes
and conjunctions all at the same time

It's how I express what's in my mind

105

So you asked what I think of you
Like an unfinished work of Art,

The artist never really ever finished that piece,
He or she is like the life force growing inside me,
They just simply think
I'm done working on this particular piece

I'm not saying you're a work of art, but
I'm not saying you aren't
You're fine as hell,
but your mind moves like an artist,

Constantly thinking wondering
when or where to start
Coming up with every possibility
your mind is brilliant like Mozart

Your actions match your words like
a fine tuned race car hugging the road's curves
I appreciate your honesty
Even though you 'n your ex bother me
Only because I admire your desire and fire
When you would speak so highly
of your relationship

No envy, just friendship,
so I listen 'n give a lending ear
Or a comment or two when you wanted me to

Don't stop talking, I'm here to listen;
We started off as friends even before we kicked it
Or before I let you stick it

You talk about your dad as if the
Greek Gods 'n Kobe had a partnership
That's something I've never witnessed

Your laidback attitude and family oriented ways
I don't know much, but that caught my eye,
and now me and
Baby Harris are here to stay

Like an architect, your characteristics
make up the blueprint
And with your passion and motivation
to learn and rebuild sh**,

I applaud you on your commitment
I don't know if you were looking for an answer like..."
I like his look 'n he got good dick

He work two jobs can clean 'n cook. Oh he a real one,
Let me catch him with my hook"
You know that's all true, however that ain't me

Whether you feel like reading or not...
this is what I think about you
After 4 years of stalling; you laying on my chest,
us just talking

I don't know everything, I doubt I ever will,
but for now,
I thank you for giving me life
I never knew I had

Inside of me a blessing from god!
Only thing I know for sure is that
I will make a mistake
But I know as long as I tell the truth,
with you,
I'll be ok

I'm not into relationships these days,

But just let me know when you need elbow space
No need to mess up what's going great
Hopefully I answered your question
P.S. See you Friday?

November 14, 2017

Heartbeat inside of me,
Your love inspires me and wrapped

Around the thought of you and
me is beyond intensifying

5:22PM

11/30/2017

Words are so important
They go hand and hand with actions
We're taught sticks and stones,
but reality is,

Those words stick and leave in my heart and in my mind
With you as my man,
I thought you were my protector and
not even in arguing,
But in you running from the truth

Things were said that not only made me feel attacked,
but broken and ashamed from the man
I thought would protect and cherish me

I just want and need for your words to be just as...
You will not be a Daddy-less daughter
You will know and grow with your dad

108

I pray that he be your first and last true love
That he never leaves or hurt you,
That you never miss a phone call,
birthday dinner or plans

That you grow to trust love and never feel heartache
Or heartbreak from your first true love
While no human is perfect,
I can only hope and pray

I teach you all the right things and
to always depend and
Rely on the lord our God
who can and will do NO wrong

10:25AM

12/10/2017

I hate you. I hate you because I still love you
I hate you because I wish I never met you
From the moment I laid my eyes on you,

Standing 6 feet tall, light brown eyes
that make me drool over you,

Arms that Comfort me in the worst storm
Vows exchanged which meant nothing
Your love seems to be nothing,
But a price tag and a cost
I thought you were my protector,

but you broke me down as you built her up
Mentally and physically,

I can't be with you, but my heart will be forever lost
I can't forgive myself for not staying strong enough

I should've fought harder 'n longer,
I should've been a better helpmate

I'm sorry for leaving you when you needed me most
, but for my baby's sake,
I had to cut you loose

You are my weakness, but I found strength in my baby
I didn't choose another man over you,
I choose my baby;
I continuously pray for you both

It hurts not seeing you hearing your voice
Laying in your arms kissing your
lips that no longer belong to me

But it's even harder just seeing
your name or picture pop up on my email screen

I didn't want to hurt you,
but I needed to start letting go
I don't know if or when I'll ever be whole,
but with my baby,
I'll grow 'n stay strong

I'm sorry I broke my promise to never leave you
But when you refused to stick around,
I was shattered inside

You pushed me away,
and all I ever wanted from you was love,
Honesty, and being in your arms

You still lie
You didn't find out from my email, but its okay,
I forgive you and I'm working
on forgiving her every day

I love you and I wish you the best,
I pray you and your soul find happiness

Still I have so much to say but
I won't hold onto my anger, hurt, brokenness, 'n
No longer that woman, but growing to be a
great God fearing mother

Stay blessed, my Paki Mia, my heart,
As you're on it for better and worse

Chapter 11

Part I

Part of me

10/21/17

roz, I cut you off because
I choose my baby over you
As much as I love you,
whenever I think about you, see you,
or talk to you,

I just cry, and that's not healthy for me or the baby
I cry because you just don't get it
This whole time you've been making it all about you
You don't want to be lonely
You don't want to be alone

You don't have anyone,
you push everyone away
You're ready to try

You told me get an abortion 'n
you would take me back 'n forget everything
Then you said if I can't have
any kids in the future that's okay

Not once asking me what I want.
What I thought
You can be so insensitive and selfish

You have no idea what it's like to take a child's life
especially one growing inside of you

You don't want me because
I'm your wife

Or because you made a huge mistake
Or because you realize I'm the love of your life.
I forgive you for cheating on me and
the mean disrespectful things you said to me

But God doesn't allow us to forget for a reason
So we know not to go back to it
I'm glad you are going back to church,
I hope it continues.

8:21PM

12/9/17

You never told me that she doesn't matter or
that I didYou said sorry,
but I never really felt you mean it
I can't give the ring back,
I'm not ready to

I need closure and even with these words,
I still don't know or think I'll find it
There's so much and I don't even know
how to say it all

I don't have anyone in my corner,
all I had was you
I thought you would be the one
I'd always talk to, the one who I could depend on

And you turned out to be the exact opposite
So now, I'm left to pick up the
pieces of not just my broken heart, but my new life
Without you, with my daughter, with a new mind

113

I'm grateful for your help, even now,
I always was; it's hard for me to look at you
Hear your voice, see your name—
anything involving you

We can keep in touch,
but I'm just not ready or able to have any type of
Conversation or anything with you

I don't know how to accept or exist
without you being my husband, my friend,
My supporter, my comforter, my protector
So it'll take some time

A lot of time, however,
we can check in from time to time and
stay in touch,

But don't ask me things right now!
I do forgive you roz, but my heart is still broken
I'm always praying for you!

12:21PM

05/12/2018

When I love, I love hard
I'm loyal, which becomes my downfall
I really don't want to give away my
heart or get involved
But it's too late for that now

You gave me life when you gave me my daughter
A perfect combination of the two of us
before there was even a US

With the most beautiful toothless smile,

She is so pure in essence and just

being in her presence,
Let's me know
God had this predestined

10:59PM

05/16/2018

Wanted-Want me
I need you to tell me you want me
Tell me you love me

Even if you don't mean it
Make me feel like I'm the only one for you,
Even if I'm only your Tuesday boo

4:23PM

06/19/2018

I don't do Subscriptions,
But keep in mind my Kind is hard to come by.

I love you, I hate you, and I love you again
How come it seems like you don't want me to win?

7:58AM

07/24/2018

Every time I think about opening up
You do something to make me think otherwise
And it could just be my own insecurities
with guys in general

So instead of my accusing and constantly asking,
I just fall back
I know you not ready for no long term
commitment, cool,

We can keep rockin' how we are,
but if along the way you ever feel like it
I'm not what or who you want in your future,
just let me know please
And we can leave it at that.

I'm not good with expression but
I hope you know
I look at you as one of my
God-given blessings

Not because you're a rebound,
but because this is the time
God allowed you and I to be now
You've given me the best gift in the
world and with that,
I've grown to know and care for you...

From regular conversation or the
little eyebrow thing you do
It's all genuine I promise
Because believe it or not,
I would have never let you in

I apologize for talking crazy way back when
But please believe me,
you are a great man and father and Yarah,
I would never take from you

I do my best to show you I care
I appreciate all you do, and when
I pull back, shut down, it's because

I feel myself getting deeper now
So I start to shut down

I genuinely feel things that
I didn't at first, but not because
I wasn't attracted to you,
but because my focus is always my main view

But now you're all that I see,
and I don't know if it's just me
If we ever choose to be,
you would never have to worry about me
I can repeat this if you'd like,
but in order for me to get it all out,
It's just easier for me when I write

I hate to see you leave, but
I do understand you are still young
and may want to have fun
So, I m not gonna nag you,

this is just me getting it out of my system
I just want to thank you and
keep letting my actions show
I appreciate you and all you do!

11:57AM

12/31/2018

Loosing me

With every stroke, I'm begging him to go deeper
With every stroke,

I'm loosing me and becoming intertwined with you 'n
every secret

117

With every stroke of my pen,
I'm determined to win

Win back everything every single piece of me
I no longer wish to lay with you and
get back the pieces of my soul that
I gave to you with every stroke,
I'm enjoying every moment

With every stroke, my soul is slowly growing dormant
With every stroke,
the devil is smiling and
I'm just trying to rearrange 'n
figure how to compartmentalize
These millions of pieces of my lives
from these millions of
Spirits that I know have inside

With every stroke, I'm focused on
pain focused on pleasure
When really it wasn't meant to be and
I'm falling into an

Abi's...continuation of my lack of communication

I was feeling fine till I let you get inside,
another piece of me gone, and to God I cry
Please don't let me to continue
down this path with a hopeless cry
Lord, hear my plea, and pray that I don't hope to die

1:09PM

12/31/2018

You healed me, but you also hurt me
Maybe god was telling me that I'm unworthy

Unworthy of love or forgiveness or

just teaching me a lesson because
I knew I should not have did this
This feeling is so crazy,
carrying the weight of someone else's baby

A fetid to be birthed, a soul's in need of purged.
Several weights to keep me down.
Screwing too many men,
now I'm empty somehow

Trying to figure it all out
Trying to drowning all of my
sorrows in this empty liquor bottle

My soul seeming so hollow
I stand in the cold as I howl at the wind,
a freak of nature God's creation
Oh lord, why did I let those men in?

Forgive me of my sin, tell the devil no more,
I don't want to play with him
Feeling so weighty, my heart cannot take it
I need a new, outlet something to help me break it

I focus on him, his word is how
I'm planning to win
Please hear my cry, please hear my plea,
please read these words,
it's my prayer to thee

Lord help me know before
I get sucked back in,
I have a daughter now,
so I need to WIN

Eyes filling with water
Heart beating harder
Stomach getting softer
Throat feeling shorter
Mind at ease

I close my eyes and find my PEACE

1:33PM

05/17/2019

What makes you NOT love me?
Be honest

All the things I do that have such thought,
"ooh's and
Awh's" behind the scenes 'n
you still don't love me
Why don't you love me!?
I'm older now, but my first love
taught me to never get comfortable
He brought to my attention my worth,
or attributes, at the time

Yet, he too did not know how to love me
Why don't you love me?

I fooled around a couple times knowing
I didn't love them
Being lied to and some thinking
I was okay with being their midnight
and day coverNo true commitment.
No for sure lover
Why don't you love me?

My first husband, yeah, he made me hungry

Introducing me to a better life,
now it's what I thirst for
He needed to live himself,
so he wounded me and
I went through hell

But I learned a lot; I pray for him still.
At first I wondered, now I know
I have growth

I admit, I did ask the Question,
"Why don't you love me?" but it was too late and
I see now

Now my daughter's father,
I should have handled him more tenderly
He has such a big heart, but very stubborn and "manly"

I know he loves me, but he'll never say it
Maybe I should give him a break, we just hooked up,
and he never wanted marriage
But still I ask, "why don't you love me?"

A man's actions should and will match his words
But the unspoken bond
we share has been brought to life in a child
that we share

I do my best to leave the past in the past 'n hopefully not
You know,
I think I often find myself asking this question
I had a child,

my daughter who I got from God and
dedicated back to God
Because I know he knows how to love me!
In and out

Intimately with only one thing on his mind,
giving him the glory and clout
He showed me how to love me
He loves me

God wants me to give in and surrender to him
When the only question I'll have is,
"What next should I do!?"
And yet he probably looks down at me and asks,
"My child, why don't you love me?"

I'm constantly struggling with my flesh
and commitment and saying yes
Father, please forgive me for I have sinned,
I know you know what I go through,
that you showed agape love

When your son Jesus picked up
that cross and on that 4th lash and a
Thorne and a half, he took those
for me and my sanity

5:05PM

05/31/2019

When sex doesn't matter,
she becomes dangerous
She becomes dangerous because
she doesn't need you
She doesn't need the things
a man might want to receive

She yearns for the creator
For knowledge
For peace
For power

122

It took some time, but that girl caught fire
She took flight and God was the one guiding her
When worldly things don't matter, she becomes a target

She becomes a target because
others no longer understand her or agree with her
She doesn't care about a new car or materialistic things.

She searches within herself for her
higher most inner being
She just one day decided to level up

7:35AM

Part II

When sex doesn't matter,
she becomes dangerous
She becomes dangerous because
she doesn't need you
She doesn't need the things
a man might want to receive

She yearns for the creator
For knowledge
For peace
For power

It took some time, but that girl caught fire
She took flight and god was the one guiding her
When worldly things don't matter, she becomes a target

She becomes a target because
others no longer understand her or agree with her
She doesn't care about a new car or materialistic things
She searches within herself for her higher most inner being
She just one day decided to level up

06/07/2019

When you look at me, what do you see?
You call me pretty
Do you see my wings?

You call me beautiful
Do I shine like rare things?
You call me strong
Do you see my tears?

You call me smart
Do you see my fears?
You call me "friend"
Do you see my loneliness?
You call me...

You call me these things and maybe more
I struggled with coming up with even one more
I don't feel worthy, I'm somewhat insecure

Mentally fragile and easily breakable,
but at the same time, still able to endure
These are my fears and more
Yet, he loves me still and in him,
I can become more
Made whole and grown to fit the mold

4:37PM

06/24/2019

Don't think you know me from reading my bio
Don't think you can control me
from being able to tell me I won't grow

Don't think I'm perfect because
I post what I want you to see
Don't think you can judge me
because you're not my creator. See?

See, don't think you know when you barely know you
Don't think you know me when
I barely know me

Trying to grab hold 'n not skip trying to ride the wave,
and instead I slip
Don't think twice when you listen with your
ears and see me with your eyes

Yes, those eyes that I know for
sure are judging when really I'm not me
Really it's all a mask you see

Really it's a charade and
we're all showing up trying to be
Accounted for at the masquerade with no luck
But don't look at a half empty cup,
just think of it as still having time

Still having luck, still getting blessed, still seeing
God is real and your faith will begin to
heal and then, Boom!
My cup runneth over
Whether I'm the one getting
blessed or being a blessing
Whether it's a gift 'n curse,
or I'm done stressing

No matter if I'm slowly
drowning and you're surviving
Don't think I'm okay because I'm not
Don't think Im happy because I smile

Don't assume I'm living because
I'm walking around breathing!
I'm just trying to find me in this
endless sea of life you see

I'm not perfect,
I have my struggles and damn
if they don't consume me
But I am fighting to be whole

I got a long list of problems,
but I'ma tell you I'm good
I have a whole list of fears that are
just waiting to take me out
I had a whole lot of doubt,
but I just canceled it all out
I have drive.

Determination24 hours every day and growing faith
So, don't count me out

This could be longer, but I'm finished drowning;
I'm swimming to the top
Even if you're not rooting for me

Just stop judging, along with all the
hate and violence please
Don't think you know me when you see me on TV
Pray for me and my safety

Don't think you know me 'cause
I'll be driving a foreign whip you see,

Don't think you know me and say
I'm acting brand new
Don't think you know me when
I'm just getting blessed to continue

to be someone else's blessing!

Don't think you know me 'Cause
I'm constantly growing!
Don't think you know me, 'cause
I prayed my struggles would be over 'n
my God showed me!

07/17/2019

Hanging tree, hanging tree
Let me see

I honestly don't know if
I can find the words as to
what you endured or as to what you heard

From the quiet snickers to the loud laughter,
what a disaster
And hanging tree,

I'm sure if you could talk your lives
Story would be more than graphic
more than drastic

From the soles of his or her feet you feel every
Empty heartbeat as you witness the blood leave

Dripping into your roots,
you two are now intertwined as
His or her last living thing;
your encounter was far from perfect,

But from your branches my ancestors
fought a little harder

Finding comfort in your every vine,
or as the wind blows the leaves,
They grab hold of a life that could be

Hanging tree, you give oxygen and bear life,
But that is not what the white man sees
Hanging tree,

he used you and your life force against me
Hanging tree, white men made you
turn against the very lives you provide air for,
You see?

Hanging tree, you were used as a
pawn in this game of life
Taken something such as a life,
but you had no choice,
It wasn't you right..?

Hanging tree, say you didn't enjoy it,
Say you wish you could fight back and re-do it
Start over and forget it all!
Hanging tree, you watched over as
If you were there to brush out the
knots in my ancestors hair,
standing when all they really
wanted was some fresh air

Hanging tree, you can't speak, but
I imagine that me taking place as your personifier,
You wouldn't disagree

You did not enjoy any of those things
Hanging tree,
I wish you could've been weak for me

12:33AM - IG ting

128

po•em

/ pō m,pōm/

Learn to pronounce

noun

a piece of writing that partakes of the nature of both speech and song that is nearly always rhythmical, usually metaphorical, and often exhibits such formal elements as meter, rhyme, and stanzaic structure.

synonyms:

verse, song, rhyme, piece of poetry, verse composition, metrical composition; rareverselet

something that arouses strong emotions because of its beauty.

What is in a poem?

It is a form of written word that has pattern and rhythm and rhyme. It can be serious or it can be fun. Poetry is as creative as you make it. Basic poetry is in verse form, called a stanza, made up of meters created by feet. The amount of lines there are in a stanza decides what type of poem is written.

What is Poetry?

Poetry is literature in meter form. It is a form of written word that has pattern and rhythm and rhyme. It can be serious or it can be fun. Poetry is as creative as you make it

Basic poetry is in verse form, called a stanza, made up of meters created by feet. The amount of lines there are in a stanza decides what type of poem is written. There can be more than one stanza to a poem and then for effect throw in a chorus and a refrain.

The stanzas can have rhythm and rhyme or just be a blank verse!

Take a look at our glossary and you will find an explanation for all sections of poetry.

Why don't you try writing a poem and enter it into one of our poetry competitions.

https://www.youngwriters.co.uk/terms-poetry

Transition to Volume II.

The shift. The shift in my life, my mind, my relationships. Dive back into my mind as I Notice/Recognize unhealthy and healthy relationships in my life. From the workplace and personal life. I've experienced the heartbreaking yet distracting woes of ludas, eros, and even storge type of love. I don't know what it is about our "Attraction to Distraction" whether it be people, things, or food. Toxic is toxic and its best to learn, reflect, and commit to change sooner or later. On many different occasions more than one you experienced my obsession and attraction to lust, hurt and pain that all steamed from my adolescent way of thinking and feeling in comparison to where my heart and mind are now.

Time to join me on a new journey, a healthier and happier journey as I experience and express my interaction and reaction with Philia, and Pragma type of love on many different levels and the way my mind began to transform and process the hurt or disappointment differently. Let's take a ride in my mind yet again for the very stylistic and simplistic way of expression while coming out of depression; time to transition into 'Love! Love. Love? Volume II.

Beware of "Love!Love.Love?", it is a bit graphic and tortured soul-like; my tale of loves lost and found. Through my eyes, through my triggered heart and mind. Before a time when I took responsibility and became aware of my own loveless patterns. In and fully consumed by my most vulnerable place; from my head which is led by my heart to paper is where it all starts. My dark and broken place. Sometimes, I come here to visit, or stay to live in a continuous moment. I can embrace it and be my best authentic creative self. Hard wired to sin. Focused on the gratitude of receiving "Right Now." Loving and usually ending up crushed, pain-filled, and over run. Ratings range from A to Z; my love felt experiences— Mentally, Physically, and Emotionally. The first book in my three-part series books of poems (The first Hundred).

Thank You
for Reading

www.ingramcontent.com/pod-product-compliance
Lightning Source LLC
Chambersburg PA
CBHW070046100426
42740CB00013B/2818